To Bessie e Da___,

Lots of Love

Janet
xx
x

ANCHOR BOOKS

INSPIRATIONS FROM SCOTLAND

Edited by

David Foskett

First published in Great Britain in 1996 by
ANCHOR BOOKS
1-2 Wainman Road, Woodston,
Peterborough, PE2 7BU

HB ISBN 1 85930 397 8
SB ISBN 1 85930 392 7

Foreword

Anchor Books is a small press, established in 1992, with the aim of promoting readable poetry to as wide an audience as possible.

The poems in *Inspirations From Scotland* represent a cross-section of style and content.

These poems are written by young and old alike, united in their passion for writing poetry.

I trust this selection will delight and please the authors from *Scotland* and all those who enjoy reading poetry.

David Foskett
Editor

CONTENTS

ONGOING

Taste life's pleasures
but beware of the traps
the unseen pitfalls increasing downward
until it gives way to total collapse

Memories confuse the picture
they distort the vision
blurring the blindness
held in the balance
a pendulum swinging

Focus the eyes on a new horizon
on a greater vision within grasp.
Cling to the right to exist
for a purpose of new life everlasting.

Catherine Dundas

CURSE ON THE MOTOR CAR

What is this rattling, smelly, noisy thing,
That's foisted on our lives?
This stinking heap of merchandise,
That everybody drives.
This conglomerate of steel and wires,
Nuts and bolts, wheels and tyres,
That guzzles gasoline and oil,
Then belches smoke and fumes to spoil,
The very air that we must breathe,
It makes my blood and body seethe,
And blaspheme such that one can't mention,
To castigate this dire invention,
O damn! This trash technology,
A curse on our ecology.

Donald Hopkins

1

UNWANTED LOVE

I loved you for years, I'm sure you must know,
I should have been stronger, and let you go
We shared some good times, and bad times too,
but even through bad times, my love was true,
I cried many a tear, but you didn't care,
for my feelings of love, you didn't share,
I lived in hope that one day you'd say
those 3 little words that would make my day,
though those words never came, I lived in hope
that some day you'd love me, helped me to cope
I'd have given you my body, heart and soul
to have your love returned was my only goal
But one day I had to break my own heart
by facing the truth, that we should part.
It was hard for me to walk away,
from the one I loved, on that sad day
I knew I had to set you free,
give you back your life,
'Twas on that day I faced the truth,
I'd never be your wife.

J Stirling

THE TRINITY

Often when I think and sit
And think of things I know and see,
I wonder when I think I've wit
Just who is God and who is me.

Then when I turn it all around
The same things that I know and see,
To that same question I am bound,
Who is the Devil,- Him or me.

On this philosophic level
The words we're using must agree,
Defining God, defining Devil,
More to the point, - defining me.

For *Myself* the point I seek,
So much of them I find in me;
Am I the link so frail and weak
In this primal *Trinity*.

Jim Laird

IN A WORLD OF WORDS

If words were forged from weapons
destruction would be oppressed
the need for communication
would take precedence instead
and wars would be forgotten
to be locked in vaults, where dust
had time to settle
As if metal turned to rust.
Generals could be poets
Soldiers carry books
Presidents and Monarchs
would perhaps be understood
and differences in cultures
would be more than black or white
a child would only be distinguished
by the language that he'd write
your enemy would listen
and then become your friend
A world where war is cured with words
Would be like Heaven's Scent.

Alan Glendinning

UNTITLED

The grass sways gently
Brushing to and fro across the craggy face
Lightly caressing as a mother would do
Across the soft features of her young
But this is no longer a person
This is a far away memory
One who was loved
And who also loved
But has now gone as the snow in the sun

Sadness encircled those who cared
Deep emotions no longer lost
Were bared for all to see
Appropriate sentiments were uttered
Some from the heart
Other merely lip service
Flowers were laid and faded away
Like the memory of the soul

As the passage of time went by
Those who endured the sadness also left
Never to meet again
As they had anticipated
Now the stones are covered with moss
Letters appear and disappear
As the grass sways gently
Gone but not forgotten?
Or simply forgotten because they have gone.

Janet Fry

A SCOTSMAN'S LAST REQUEST

When I am far away my dreams they wander,
Back to the land where I was born and bred.
Memories of heather covered moorlands,
And majestic soaring eagles overhead.

Waterfall cascading down the hillsides,
Where stately deer are roaming wild and free,
And pipers play the tunes of hope and glory,
Yes that's the place that I would rather be.

But here I am in far off foreign places,
Dreaming of the things I used to do,
And when I'm lying here and I am dying,
There's just one thing that I must ask of you.

Take me home and lay me neath a Rowan tree,
A bunch of purple heather in my hand,
And at my headstone plant a single thistle,
And at my feet a lowly piper stand.

Sheena Ingram

IN A JAM-JAR

Ripe fruits fallen
shocked from their branches by
full-blown assault of the
autumn wind.
Rescued by
tender hands, and
conserved
for later recovered
sweetness, as
many a slice of
dried-up crusty bread
would testify.

Annie Glass

STEVEN ALEXANDER

I shouted at you today
My boy, just four years old.
I said you mustn't do those things
You must do as you're told.

I shouted at you today
Big tears filled up your eyes
You looked at me to reassure
And soothe away your cries.

I shouted at you today
Your little mouth turned down
The usual smile that lights your face
Replaced by a saddened frown.

I shouted at you today
Head bent and facing down
Pulling at fingers, feet turned in
Just staring at the ground.

Then; I smiled at you today
Your face transformed to gold
I loved you still - I always will
My boy, just four years old.

Brenda Graham-Flanagan

TO BE HOMELESS

I feel as if no-one cares.
I feel ashamed to be homeless.
I used to have a home; family and work
But now I have nothing.

I beg for food; money and somewhere to stay
But still no-one cares.
I wish I had everything as it was.
I would not be out in the cold like this.
Sleeping in doorways and in cardboard boxes.
That is my life now.

Elizabeth Anne Kelso

TOO LATE FOR TEARS?

Animals keep running,
What are they running from?
Children, they are crying for food
But they have none.

The rain forests, they are dying
Even as I write this song,
The ozone layer is giving up
Doesn`t everyone know what's wrong?

People, they just turn their backs
On everything that's said
Ignoring all the possibilities
that someday we'll all be dead.

The pain and anguish the earth suffers
Isn't very fair,
It's meant to have some TLC.
From those that live there.

How long will people go on?
How long before they see?
That money can't buy everything,
Are humans a dying breed?

Lena Poulos (14)

ANGELS AT MY FEET

The river sent me angels
Angels at my feet
The sun that leant
And kissed the waters
Ever dancing lips
Returned in kind
Angels
Angels at my feet.
They danced the motion
Of the water
Rhythms of the deep
They sprinkled sun kisses
And sun wishes
And secrets blind
And I saw them dance
Those angels
Angels at my feet.
Silently the sun that leant made
His final bow
And as he gave his parting
Kiss the angels bade me well.
'Seek the time the sun
Doth kiss the water's ever
Dancing lips
And there will be angels
Angels at thy feet'.

Bea Last

AUTUMNAL YOU

I thought I'd dreamt of everything,
Of leaf-strewn paths both wide and deep.
That you were sitting at my feet,
Of river banks and willow trees
And alders shimm'ring in the breeze.

8

But then I knew what I had done -
I'd walked those paths both deep and wide
And you were walking at my side
But I was one that did not see
Those river banks and willow trees
And alders shimm'ring in the breeze.

W Williamson

TIN-BATH

Rent, ten shillings and sixpence for my
cottage by the sea.
Bread and jam, dripping on bread, the table
is set for tea
On the fire we place a log, a chill is in the air
Darkness descends upon us, there's little
time to spare.

The candles cast their shadows, all around
the room
The old tin bath, comes in at last, we'll fill
it very soon
The pans are placed above the fire, bath-water
they contain
Some collected from the well, the rest is
from the rain.

One by one we have a bath, the cleanest goes in first
The biggest person sits quite still, in case
the bath should burst
The water then has one more use, to soak
the clothing in
Because the next day's Monday, wash-day
for those within.

Christine Thain

I'VE HATED HER SINCE THE DAY SHE WAS BORN

It didn't come as a surprise,
When he shouted those words,
I'd always known it somehow,
And it had ceased to hurt.

He said it with such venom,
Bitterness and force,
He wanted it to sting me,
To hurt me; but of course.

I stood and didn't answer,
I took it - almost with pride.
It didn't matter what he thought,
I had nothing to hide.

But hate is such a strong thing,
To feel for anyone,
Especially a baby,
Fresh out of the womb.

And then to let it fester
On as the baby grew.
To act as if things were normal,
As if no one ever knew.

Then to blurt it out,
As if I wasn't there -
The third party, unfamiliar,
Just shows he didn't care.

Marian Silvester

WORDS FOR MY LOVED ONE

My special flower the first night we met.
I'll never forget when we danced together
I was hoping it would last forever
When we went outside the night was so
calm and to me my darling you're as pure
as a new born lamb, the moon and stars were dancing
in the night stay in my arms as I want to hold you so tight. You have
long beautiful dark hair,
with skin so fair, lips as red as a Christmas cherry
you have a heart as warm as the sun
you are my only one. Though at
times we may be miles apart there
will always be a place for you here
in my heart, you will always be
my friend until my life comes to an
end. May God bless you for being
so true.

Duncan Maclean

HOME HILLS

I've just returned from far-off climes,
Still reeling with the thrill of seeing new mountains and meeting new friends.
Amongst a familiar landscape again which feels like an old acquaintance;
Permanent, resolute, forgiving (I'm sorry I've been away so long),
There when I need it.
I see the land with new eyes and its vibrancy excites me.
I feel humbled and apologetic
That I've not noticed the beauty of that bracken-covered hillside until now.
Hills, trees, river - it's good to see you all again.
Lochnagar stands proud and defiant (as ever) against its rural foreground,
And to the north, the high Cairngorm plateau entices.
How I love this country.

Leslie Fraser

FORBIDDEN PARK

Passing through a park by a river on a
Dull December day,
The clouds take form in their mastery
of a resurrection way,
A day in a bed of thought which fills
An inner sanctum,
A prayer from which I have never fallen,
Wet banks and goodbye grass which dwell
In lost domains,
Forgiving trees with timeless cause as the
Water rains,
I will begin to see,
My eyes lifted by your sombre hand,
The essence of life will come forth from
This forbidden land,
Grey is the face of beginning for this
Disguise is graced,
And no further from this haven may man be misplaced.

Lisa O'Brien

WHAT ARE YOU LOOKING AT?

Don't do that they say, as if I listen anyway.
I walk on by with my head held high, in my mind *Shut Up* is all I want
to say.
Then there comes the thought of people that are poorer than me,
starving, homeless, scared or hurt but what can I do, I'm just me.
Trees blowing just like a dream, for how long is what I want to know.
People today, just toss their head as if to say (not me can't do nowt)
It sure does get you thinking, when life's not your way.
For some people that's every day.
Imagine thinking that way every day, tears roll down your cheek,
People stare and leave you no choice but for you to say 'what are you
looking at?'

Lisa Bertram

PANSIES
(Heartsease)

In the quiet moments of the day
when the work is over
and the children are in bed,
and all is silent, save the
ticking of the clock - I think of you,
and am transported to other days
when love's bright face was young.

We would wander hand in hand
among the blossoms, and you
would fill my arms with posies -
roses for love, carnations for affection
and pansies, that our hearts
would know no pain.

Crammed into a pot they stood,
a raggle - taggle bouquet, spilling
petals on the sun - splashed sill,
filling the room with fragrance,
a token of our love.

How fleeting is happiness - for you
were much too wise and beautiful
to escape God's wistful eye
and when He called your name
you answered.

Today I gathered flowers,
brought you roses and carnations
and laid them on the brown,
unyielding earth . . .
but I, for my heart's ease
have the pansies still
in a pot, in the sun, on our window-sill . . .

Fiona Walker

ELEGY FOR CHILDHOOD

Remember the parks and little wynds
Where, as children, we played.
Our lives were full of youthful dreams
Our ambitions and plans were laid

Life seemed slow, so long ago
And endless summers of sun.
The Shore Terrace baths
Were good for a laugh
As we ducked and dived and swam

In the old Arcade, there was lemonade,
Roasting chickens and toys,
And Champion, the wooden horse,
Gave rides for the girls and boys

On Saturday, we made our way
To Wallace's, my parents, my brother and me
For bridies and chips and fizzy drinks
And silver pots of tea

We'd sit in the dark, at the Forest Park
Watching the drama unfold
On wooden seats that groaned and creaked
These memories are made of gold

On Balgay Hill, I found my thrill
The first kiss I ever took,
In that little park, just before dark
Was like a page from a romance book

Although they've gone and I've moved on
In my memory, they'll always be.
Now and then, they'll flow from my pen
And once again I'll see
Those childhood places and untied laces
And the little boy that was me.

Scott Martin

HER LEFT FOOT

My wife has got a sore left foot, she's had it for some years
There's been the odd occasion when it's brought her near to tears
So she went to the doctor to see what he would say
He examined it, and said to her
'This is your lucky day'
We've got a chap just up the road, whose specialty is feet
And after he's examined it he'll fix you up a treat
He's good with *heels*, he's good with *soles*, especially good with *toes*
Just remember though what he decides, whatever he says goes

So they did an operation and asked her how it feels
They said 'It's looking pretty good, you'll soon be in high heels'
This made her quite ecstatic, she didn't mind the pain
To think that she could wear her thirty pairs of shoes again

Alas! Things haven't gone to plan, her foot is still quite sore
And now it's broader than it was, a half an inch or more
That presents new problems, a challenge she must meet
For now she hasn't any shoes that fit upon her feet
Of course she's down, she's in the dumps
She's really got the blues
And what of the dilemma of sixty useless shoes?

J S Glass

CONTENPLATO

Continents are nothing
when melodious gods
are in tune with mortal singing
Beauty is harmony
harmony is friendship
always seek out new melodies

Carolyn Davies

TO YVONNE

When the dawn breaks, you light the day;

When the mist rises, I banish your fears;
When the sun shines, you make me laugh;
When the thunder cracks, I hear your voice of calm;
When the lightning strikes, you understand;
When the rain pours, I wipe away your tears;
When the wind blows, you breathe into me a sweeter life;

When the sun sets, we share our dreams . . .

C W Lush

THINGS OF THE NIGHT

The sun's away, the moon it beckons
to the man who dares to the man who reckons
The witches and charmers a wander this night
to scare poor travellers with all of their might.
Stay inside the circle all will be well
awake my friend to hear this deathly bell,
Its toll so loud strong and scary
look out behind for the man's who's hairy
Werewolf is what he's been named
A pact with the Devil, a poor soul framed
Try not to listen try not to sigh.
Run away very fast and very hard
This man's playing with the devils card
A cry in the forest upon the witching hour
try not to stop or it'll grasp you in its power
it's getting close I can feel its breath
or is that just the fear of death.

Brutus

16

ANAR-KAY

Kay's sitting in her chair
Like the queen of Timbuktu
And she's shouting for her dinner
Which she wants right noo
Doogies running after her
Like a mad, demented moose
While Kay rants and raves
About the colour of her juice
Oh it's nearly ten o'clock
The house goes deathly silent
And if there's as much as a peep
Kay may get violent
Cos at ten o'clock is the news
Kay's chosen religion
And nothing gets as much attention
As that old television
Doogies in the kitchen baking
Kay's favourite Scottish scones
While because of the price of butter
Dear old Kay moans
And anyone who goes in
May get a quiet hello
And her mouth will stay tightly shut
Until your cheerio
Doogie will run around forever
Where Kay says he goes
So what puts the girn on Kay's face
I don't really know.

Wesley Burns

STONE

Things are always going on
Nothing ever changes
People keep on moving on
Constant rearranges
Angels, demons, in my head
What the hell should I do?
Lovers, sinners in my bed
The air is turning blue.

Life and death, it's always the same
When you go, you're gone
Everything just now seems tame
Day and night seem long
Feeling useless and abandoned
Feeling hurt and alone
People just don't understand
Living life like a stone.

Craig Thompson

MOONSCAPE

As our Earth home turns,
and daylight lights our lives again,
the yellow lunar orb fades in the west,
while in the eastern sky, the giant star
that keeps us, colours the heavens orange red.

The fragile system that sustains our lives is changing now, thanks to
thoughtless actions
caused by human greed.
If we don't change our lifestyle soon,
the polar caps will shrink, the oceans rise,
and this green island in the solar world
will turn into a barren rock,
a mirror image of the moon.

David Todd

THE MORAY COAST

All along the Moray coast,
The sun shone with colours bright,
Waves breaking on the shore,
With all their strength and might.

My tired feet were bare,
No shoes upon my feet,
The warm sand gently caressing,
A sensation that's hard to beat.

It brought back childhood memories,
Of playing in the sand,
Building sand-castles, and the like,
With my brothers giving a hand.

An old lady passes me by,
Suitably adorned in a summer frock,
Her hat tilting, above her brow,
Like a buckie on a rock.

In the distance a lone fishing boat,
Returning with the fruits of the sea,
Home to the safety of their loved ones,
As I'm sure they're glad to be.

All my worries, my fears,
Seemed no longer to exist,
My mind and my body,
Truly relaxed . . . what bliss.

As the sun gently fades away.
The darkness now my host
I'll wait for another day,
To enjoy this Moray Coat.

Ian A Little

WHY?

Why must we all conform to type
Behold the masses out to win
The single thought which is our right
To be ourselves it seems a sin

Why must we always keep that rule
The law's society expect obeyed
Restricting freedom as in a pool
A measured depth where life is played.

Why must we all be so sedate
Our feelings bottled deep inside
Afraid to start a new debate
Or labelled rebel with view too wide.

Why must we always count the cost
Withhold the gift that freedom brings
The spirit tamed, expressions lost
So sad the bird with its clipped wings.

Kathleen Thornton

FALKLANDS WAR

The roses we planted last autumn
Will bloom every year from now on;
But I lie here in a distant land
My life and my love all gone.

Remember me my darling
As you gently place each bloom
'Neath that shady tree where we first loved
Beneath the August moon.

Please forgive and forget any heartache
I caused you, in those few years we shared
And do not grieve forever
For you life must go on.

And when our children grow up
I hope that you will explain
Why I'm not there to share their joys,
Their sorrows or their pain.

Adeline J Haythorne

A TONGUE IN CHEEK HISTORY OF PAISLEY

When *Mirren* and his 'band of monks' went walking by the Cart,
Said Mirren 'Get your shovels out and let us make a start . . .
And let us build our Abbey here
Right in Paisley's heart!'

Soon houses sprung up all around and people had to eat.
So they set about planting out
Fields of barley, oats and wheat.
And fetched their drinking water home
From stand-pipes in the street.

Some cottage dwellers stayed at home
To weave 'The Paisley shawl'
Then tenements began to rise
So stately, high - so tall.
Then Coats and Clark had great mills built
Providing work for all.

Now if Saint Mirren should come back
To our dear town once more . . .
Oh! Please - go down to Love Street . . .
And teach them how to score.

Jane Owen

RED DRESS

The ooh - la- la dress in cancan red.
Low cut, designed to reveal.
Was purchased with a deeper need.
Than mere desire to acquire.

It oozed femininity in its ribbon straps.
As the shoulders they caressed.
And the wind wafted movement of the skirt, gave a womanly feel.
The top gave a hint of soft breast.

It's pleasing, moulding, closeness.
Sensually clasped the body in a folding embrace.
And the reflecting luxurious silk sheen,
Sent a maidenly flush to the face.

It scored high on the feel good factor.
Providing an emotional crutch.
A confidence booster, a pick me up,
When life proved a touch too much.

For all its vibrant beauty.
It never received public acclaim.
For it never left the bedroom.
And was only seen outlined by the mirror's frame.

The wearer alone saw it
Stood at the mirror to preen.
No matter, if the wearer did it justice.
Only through one pair of eyes was it seen.

The dress was a dress to dream in.
Not for the realities of life.
For the solitary make-believe mannequin.
Shut away from every day strife.

Patricia Scott

A WHISPERED CARESS

A whispered caress
That's how it started
The night when you told me
We would never be parted

You told me you loved me
Would always be mine
That we'd be together
Until the end of time

Your breath brushed my neck
Your words touched my soul
Your lips kissed my mouth
My mind lost control

You won me completely
I was totally yours
I gave myself to you
That night on the moors

Now I'm left on my own
My youthful dream shattered
My spirit is broken
My heart bruised and battered

You've moved to another
Who's young and impressed
By your silver tongued words
And your whispered caress

Elizabeth Wilson

GRUNNIE'S NEW PUP

Ma Grunnie's got a new pup - a richt bonnie beast
It's jist at yon awkward age fin yer slippers mak a feast
It's chawed its wye thro the P & J, the Sunday Post an a
An the ither nicht it took ben 'e lobby wi the People's Freen in its jaw

Noo Grunnie kept her as she wis the only quine oot o six
Bit noo her brithers are awa she fair gets up tae tricks
Grunnie his ither dogs as she maks 'eir lives pure hell
She bites 'eir lugs, jumps on 'em or trails 'em by the tail

She niver sics tae gang ootside she needs a gie bit shovin
She jist loves tae hae a snooze lying in the rayburn's naithmist oven
There she lies wi 'er heid stickin oot, a nice and snug
Wakin ilka noo an 'en tae hae a chaw at 'e rug

She's aye sae pleased tae see ye fan ye gang intae Grunnie's hoose
She wags 'er tail an rins roon yer feet - scupperin like a moose
We ca her 'Flossie' - She's a West Highland - a richt Terier by name
The only thing rang is - Grunnie winna let ma tak her hame

Maureen Birnie

SOMETIMES

Sometimes I get so angry
Sometimes I feel so bad
But some things I would never change
Without you I'd be sad.

Sometimes you make me scream
Sometimes you make me shout,
But I'm always glad you're with me
It's what life is all about.

Sometimes you make me laugh
Sometimes you make me cry,
Sometimes I feel so proud of you
I know we'll all get by

You know I'll always love you both
Of that you can be sure
This daughter and this son of mine
I couldn't have wished for more.

Marlene Noble

NIGHT

In the dead of night
By heavenly power
No glimmer of light
At the midnight hour
No colourful sight
Far less waking sound
Life's put to flight
By sky or ground
By power and might
In a magic chime
I cannot blight
This special time
My throat is tight
Short is my breath
All senses slight
But far from death
I see a kite
The hawk of dawn
Upon my right
In the light of morn

Alasdair Cowie

UNTITLED

A touch is why it started
Who knows where it might end
I can't say what will happen
When my broken heart might mend
I want so much to hold you
To tell you what I'm thinking
Then you smile and say hello
And ask me what I'm drinking
I know it's only part of the game
You've said it all 1000 times before
But I can feel you watching me
When I walk through the door
So I'll be back tomorrow
Even if on wobbly knees
Then I'll smile and say again
'One cappuccino please . . .'

M Deuchars

SEA VIEW

Sitting on the golden sand looking out to sea
What a beautiful sight it fills my soul with great unease
In the far distance I can see a range of mountains
Shimmering in the noon day sun
There is a strong offshore wind blowing all around
Sandpipers scurrying all around, seagulls landward bound
Children busily building sandcastles filled with a happy glee
Ships sailing outwards to deepsea to deliver their cargoes to
foreign lands
Oh! I wish it were me: sailing, sailing into the breeze out to
deep sea
Just like those ships which glide through the sea with a majestic
ease

Richard Connal

THE MOUNTAIN

You stand so proud, so elegantly
Like a magnet people are drawn to you
Your gentle features from a far
Disillusion the eyes of the eager

From the big concrete worlds we come
Selfishly thinking we will win every battle
With our weapons we attack you
So determined, so desperate.

You let us enter your forsaken kingdom
With mother nature on your side
Like humans she too can be unpredictable
In one blink she sees us into another dimension

Monstrous mist swirling, lurking
Crags with teeth foaming at the mouth
Rivers flowing, biting, snarling
Sheer drops with bottomless bottoms

In darkness you've no lights to shine
No signs to lead us into a civilisation
It is then that we realise it's your territory
And for the first time we feel weak and defeated

You've stood, you've watched, you've survived
Like our braveheart you've conquered
Time has passed but nothing has changed
Like the wind you remain mysterious

Catriona Louise McNicoll

THE SEA AT NIGHT

The sea at night is calm and cool
Like a sheet of glass
Not a crack, not a dent,
Not a single flaw.
Not a seagull squawking,
Not a tall ship sailing.
The sea at night, perfect in every way.

The twilight moon shines on the sea
Like light on a mirror.
Not a shimmer, not a shake,
Not a single flaw,
Not a wave crashing,
Not a child playing.
The sea at night, perfect in every way.

Emma Catignani (10)

DON'T CONTROL ME

Don't tell me what to do,
You can't rule my life
You can't control me
You'll only ruin my life.

If I want your help
I'll ask you to
But don't control me
I've never done anything to you.

Why won't you leave me be?
Why can't you leave me alone?
You've got your own life
And I've got mine

Sarah Grigor

ROUGH JUSTICE

It happened one day, when my good wife espied,
A young fellow about whom, she cruelly lied,
When into their affair, I had properly pried,
To find that for me, her love had truly died.

I wanted him gone; 'Get lost,' she cried
She would not recant, though God knows, I tried,
So I shot the bitch dead, that's how she died,
Then I went to the pub, and came back cross-eyed.

I packed up my bag, to catch me a train,
A great many thoughts, raced through my brain,
Loss of memory, is a good trick to feign,
And if it came to the worst, I could plead insane.

The policemen were kind, as I listened so bland,
My wife was dead, and the murder was planned,
By her lover who was caught, with the gun in his hand,
I supported their case, when I took the stand.

The gun was for me, that's what he said,
He would give me, a bellyful of lead,
My innocence was clear, from the tears that I shed,
The jury believed me, and they hanged him instead.

It's a wonderful life, down by the Med,
Of worry and care, I have not a shred,
The wife's insurance, provides plenty bread,
And a cracking young blonde, is sharing my bed.

Eric Forbes

VERONICA

Soft as summer's morning air
fresh as morning dew
An angel sent from Heaven above
My reaching thought of you

Roses like the lady blooms
their fragrance haunts the air
Cascading down the slender stem,
your soft and gentle hair

Twinkling are the stars at night
Seen glowing in the sky
A sparkling sight of laughter bright,
just like your lovely eyes

Standing tall above the flock
Kindness shines like beacon bright
To warn of danger from the rocks
In dark despair, a guiding light

Pure mind, so clean but simple
Stout heart, so firm but true
Faint smile, with trace of dimple
My visioned thoughts of you

Shapely form, your clientele
would make a father wince
To ruin the lives of noble lords
In glory, a crown prince

Born to be a Gigolette
with act so smart and cute
No loving wife, a wasted life
A scheming prostitute

Bob Anderson

DROWNING

You asked me in our early years, how come I knew so much,
Flattered and flustered I nearly cried, I loved you then, I loved your touch.
Your floppy cakes I raised to perfection as my mother showed me how,
The pants you sewed and still left a hole, I laugh on reflection now.
We climbed some hills and walked many miles, I taught you to keep pace,
As long as you finished whatever you started, you quickly learned not
                                                                to race.

Abseiling weekends; you really thought I could fly,
The haunting face I've spent years trying to erase and leave behind,
                                                keeps on asking me why.
You struggled with simple tasks that I secretly thought so silly not to
                                                have known,
Planting vegetables and gorgeous flowers that you wanted the world to
                                                be shown.
Being so proud at the carnival when you won a round of shots,
The prize having been the only evidence of this event you got.

For hours on end I showed you how to multiply and divide correctly,
Your unconcealed adoration of me making me feel like a queen, aptly.
The tennis champion you wanted to be, but my champion you were,
                                                without the glory,
Now you are gone and it's quite a different story.
My heart aches this broken organ wasting away,
So many things you will never know, I never got to say.

For teaching you to swim, I could never admit, for the way you thought
                                                of me,
This one thing that took you away, the water don't you see,
Swimming was the one act that would have kept us together,
I never learned, you never knew, so now in this dry land we'll never
                                                be as one forever.

Michelle Crawford

31

WINDOW

Looking out my window
Like a plant that didn't grow
I see a play park that never was
Places where the ghosts may be
Ghosts whose faces we will not see.

I can see my garden that didn't grow
Dead daffodils, overgrown weeds
Plastic cups and rusty knives
Nearby there is a busy road
The car fumes killed my seeds
The engines killed human lives

I used to see trees and woods
Then they did a moonlight flit
Replaced by the new houses
The green leaves have gone far
Now it's just bricks and mortar.

What I see changes almost every day
Yet, to live in the way we are used to
It could be that it's better this way
My garden couldn't survive outside
However the plants can grow inside
One day I will see my garden grow
When I'm looking into my window.

Karen Reid

THE FINAL JOURNEY

When I took my last breath on this earth and finally closed my eyes.
The light surrounded me and I was guided up towards the skies,
I saw the beautiful rainbow and all the colours so true,
The violet, yellow, indigo, the red, the orange and the blue.
A golden light stepped forward - 'Follow me.' Was his command.

'Don't be afraid.' He whispered and gently took my hand
I have many friends here now and loved ones who passed before.
There is peace, healing and tranquillity and I'm in no pain no more.
So dry your eyes dear friends and do not grieve for me,
For happy smiles and laughter is all I want to see.
I'll be close by, near you every day.
I'll send you all love and peace to guide you on your way.

Gill Graham

FLANDERS' POPPY

It lay, a tiny pool of blood,
a Flanders' poppy grimed with mud,
bent pin with broken plastic head,
lost in action as we mourned the dead,
staining red the concrete flags,
when it rained
and poured.

The eleventh hour of the eleventh day
advanced, stood still, then marched away,
like the old men with fading ribbons
and shining memories of the Somme and Mons,
some fewer every year,
to remember those
who paid the price
so long ago.

It lay, that sodden scrap of red,
mute tribute to the silent dead,
till stretchered up by teeming torrents,
then left abandoned
in the gutter.

Ronald W McDonald

UNCERTAIN FUTURE

I canna find ma place in life
I canna find ma role
I dinna ken far I belong
I canna find ma Goal

I dinna ken fit I shid dae
To earn ma pennies day by day
I dinna ken far I shid ging
Please help me on my way

A need tae find a guidelin licht
I need tae find ma callin
I'm feelin like I canna hud on
I'm feelin like I'm fallin

I wander fit'll become o me
I wander far I'll end
I wish I kent fit I'll be
Some help wid be a Godsend

I hope that when I'm old and dead
Or lying dying in ma bed
I'll be able tae look back and laugh
An hae this chiselled as my epitaph

Here lies me as stiff as a post
Wee a bit o luck I'm nae a ghost
Although I never kent fit I wanted to be
The success I hid surprised even me

Peter Forbes

YOU PRETEND

Even though you're near me
We're still so far apart
Your body is here with me
But someone else has your heart

You pretend to love me
In each and every way
But we're just drifting apart
Slowly - every single day

Maybe it would be better
If I just let you walk away
Because it will only get worse
If you thought you had to stay

It's no use pretending
That we can stay together
I guess I now know
That nothing lasts forever

J Somshor

RACISM

Why do others hate
Others in a different state?
There's nothing wrong if you're black
or white.
Or if you're deaf or have no sight
It's their problem thinking this way
They'll realise one day.
But if they don't, then just forget
that comment or threat.
So just ignore
because you're worth much more.

Michelle Ann O'Donnell

AGEING

Old age is something that comes to us all,
The healthy weak, small, and the tall,
It's like life's ups and downs,
That miss none on us,
So look forward to it with a grudge.
For when we reach that stage,
We should never misjudge,
As a lifetime we've had to learn wisdom and trust,
Like all human beings there is sometimes a flaw
If we look close enough that flaw's in us all,
As nobody is perfect,
Most of us know,
So look forward to old age with a little more glow.

Pat Trixie Ashcroft

HOW THINGS CHANGE

When you're a girl and 14 years old,
Your thoughts start to change
And the truth unfolds.

You like different things,
different people, different places,
You understand homelessness, poverty and races.

The colour of people
White, black and brown
The truth makes you happy
And the lies make you frown.

The colour of people is not what amounts,
The person inside is what really counts.

Frances Laurenson

MOVING ON

Moving on is a part of life,
A stirring of adventure deep inside,
When at last you spread your wings,
And leave your cares behind.

Moving on with the sands of time,
It will swallow you up if you let it,
But fear not for there is nothing to fear,
The essence of life is not on the line.

Moving on with each passing day,
As the seasons and years roll by,
Until at last you decide to remain,
And let life pass by your way.

Sandra Milton

THE BRAES

Upon this hill,
I sit so high,
I gaze above,
Towards the sky
As I look down,
Towards my feet,
I see a line of,
lights so neat,
Oh if I could lift
Them in my palm,
But after all
I am just a man

Hugh MacMonagle

37

USELESS LOSS

The people of this world, never stop to think
Everytime they fight they get closer to the brink
Of escalating friction, the dangers of war.
Why do we do it? What is it for?

Death and destruction, misery and woe
'Tis not the opponent, it's us that's the foe
Send off our boys, to battle in the fields
To face guns and bullets, not swords and shields.

Hundreds and thousands and millions and more
Lying still and lifeless, they're finished with gore
Their souls are in heaven, their bodies are dead
Covered are their corpses with poppies so red.

Why send them to start with, it isn't our war?
Kuwait, or to Bosnia, it's hardly next door
Just national pride, 'See how hard we are'.
Our boys still get killed, so let's stop!

Ricky Henderson

A LOVE THAT LASTS

With a love that lasts forever more,
You're the one that I adore.
I hope we won't drift apart,
You always have a place in my heart.

Wherever in the world that you may be,
I hope that you always love me.
Whatever happens in our lives.
I hope our love always survives.

Whatever I say whatever I do,
Don't forget that I love you.
I know that love does not last forever,
But I hope that we will stay together.

Whatever trouble we both go through,
I want you to know I always love you.
Every time I see your face.
My heart suddenly starts to race.

Edward Tumath

UNTITLED

I glance through the misty scene
and see love and hate.
My eyes follow yours
but never meet.

I clear the mist,
but it comes again,
thicker.

I turn away from the coalescence into the haze,
everything blurred in front of me.

I tremble uncontrollably
though nothing of me moves.
Until I dare to turn, again.

I glance through the misty scene
and see love and hate,
my eyes follow yours,
but never meet,
again.

Kirsteen McDonald

APRIL THE COMPROMISER!

A gorgeous eve in April
with the sun just blindin' in
an aathing in the world aroond
a joy an withoot sin,
but since a started this wee rhyme,
a sudden smirrh o rain
has rendered dark the countryside -
it's peltin doon again!
But ere we've time ti see the time
the hale scene's changed like fun
an although the rain keeps fa'in doon -
above it shines the sun!

Andrew A Duncan

COLOUR BLIND

My love is just the same
Open your heart and let me in
Is my colour to you a sin?
We're all the same colour
Under our skin.
Is my desperation
a cry on the wind?
How could I be so blind
to think you were different?
The colour thing's
all in your mind.
I'm the same race
The human one,
Believe in your heart
Which is as red as mine,
Don't be colour blind.

David Baldie

STRESSES

I've washed it, I've combed it
I'm getting quite distraught
Of all the battles in my life
'Tis the biggest one I've fought
I've waved it, I've curled it
I've crimped it with tongs
I've plastered it with lotions
You can imagine how it 'Pongs'
I've pinned it up with 'Kirby Grips'
And curlers rolled up tight
It doesn't matter what I do
I still end up a fright
I've cut it, I've bleached it
A glorious shade of blonde
But what I need to make it nice
Is a magician with a wand.
I've conditioned it and permed it
Until I'm in a 'Tiz',
Yet when I rise in the morning
It's still a mass of frizz.
I've had advice from 'Experts'
'Agony Columns' in the news
I really cannot win at all
Who'd be in my shoes?
At last a man had the answer
It's a wonder I didnae 'Twig'
He handed me a parcel
And in it - You've guessed -
- A Wig -

Anne Winnie

PEOPLE PASSING

As I stand at my till,
People pass, and I know they will,
Make idle chat about the weather,
But not really caring, not wanting to blether,

As they have much more important things to do
Than waste time, talking, to little old you.

As they are holding up the queue
That is getting so much longer too.

In people's eyes, I am no brain,
A 'cash assistant' is always a pain.
But I do work hard, and earn my pay
No matter what anybody else may say,

Because despite what they may cry,
There's more to me than meets the eye.

I am quite clever and funny too,
The job is just in order to do,
What everyone else would also try;
To earn some cash so that I can buy,

Things I feel that I do need,
And also something for me to read.

So read this poem, and do take heed,
Don't treat us like dirt, when you feel the need.
Shop assistants are people too,
Show respect, like we do you.

Gillian Doig (16)

THE GENERAL SYNOPSIS

In the January night so black,
no glimmer of a star,
no hope of moon.
Far above the heaving ocean,
tropical scents float on warm breezes,
to collide against the frost of polar air.

Twisting in a mighty vortex,
two giants clinched in battle.
They brush the water's ebony skin,
exhaling briny vapour as they spin,
cloaked in an ink-black mantel,
sky and sea as one.

Dark cyclonic beast,
you speed across the void;
to claim as yours, a drifting ship,
against the will of men.
Bearing down upon the decks
to break the delicate spine.

The body sways on tumbling tide,
rolling closer to the land,
to drift not left or right
of this Old Rock that we call home.
Now oil flows like blood
around the foot of Fitful Head.

A withered dawn breaks through the dark
waves splash upon the pane.
Pressed under dense covers,
I lay and wait
in my tiny house,
on the brink of the ocean.

Rebecca Moritz

THE SLAUGHTER

Lyin' in yer bed asleep, the oors the seen flee bye,
Bit things gin on in deed o' night it niver tik yer eye.
The fish they sweem in great big lumps, they're easy meat for a,
Bit half o' them that come aboord gin straight back o'er the waa.

Conservation, 'ats fit they ask, they fight for't here ashore,
Bit ence afloat they seen forget an' its oot the ither door.
The Slaughter's fit I'd caa it, its simple as can be,
For half the fish that come aboord are dumped back in the sea.

Gone are the days fin men wid say, 'Ats enough ess wik,'
Noo it's 'Bide a bittie langer an' line oor pooches deep'.
Times are comin' fan they'll say, 'Wi did nae realise'.
Fit will wi dee wee nae fish left? Ging an' fish the skies?

Men o' God some caa them sael, ti them a noo beseech,
Mak yer stand firm for the truth an' practise fit ye preach.
The Good Book his the answers, they kaen that for a fact,
Bit fits the pint o' reading it, if on it they dinna act?

Achange o' heart, at's fit wi need, am sure ye a kin tell,
Fin nae langer will the motto be, 'Love comes in o'er the rail,
Behind the scenes ye've hid a look, the sad story ye've been told,
The fish they kaen nae better, bit we kaen its greed o' gold.

Each skipper his his point o' view, they see it different wies,
Bit few 'ill hae their answers, fan Judgement Day arrives!

Billy Wyllie

KNOW NOT I

Know not I why rainbows in translucent and wonder colour are in my sky.
Know not I why men have to die in sodden mud beneath their feet for
something that is not theirs to have and to hold and say 'Tis mine! And cherish
till all be black once more, when rainbows shed their colours for the mystery
beyond where the light truly shine for purpose.

Know not I why the little babies cry and people walking pass them by with not a flutter of an eye, glazing fixed at horizontal skies, 'We see no evil!' No not I why man do not see beyond their horizontal skies when all around them the little babies cry and die! Is't perhaps I that are blind? But though their eyes may shine their truth, my eyes are shining other truths. Which I must search for till all the lights shine on mine, thine be, no not I why anything should cry or die or hover in my sky. Goodbye!

M F B Makay

WINTER'S CHILD

Push me down your river, floating aimlessly along,
Clutching at the sky, praying it won't fall,
Winter calls, lovers part, blistering weather returns,
Boy returns to winter pastime, collecting logs for the fire,
Longing for the sun to bask on his face once more.

Chapped lips, frosty fingers, rag-tag clothes,
Numbness overcomes his tired, battered, fatigued body,
Child wishes to play, cannot due to circumstances,
Mother lies in bed, still she cannot speak,
Tired lethargy gained from hardship,
Her grey skin melts into a bleak surrounding.

Father has gone, lost forever,
Forever with the old times,
Child is worried bearing the burden of life,
Holding in his hand a power, life or death,
He must be strong or they will perish.

Sitting by the frozen stumps,
Child wonders what will become,
Joyous sun where, never to return,
Mother lies dying, I will surely follow,
Life is ending this cruel winter.

Paul Dudley

THE LAST FAREWELL

He lives silent and entrapped within his mortal shell,
The only sign of suffering in his pain-filled eyes,
Tears roll down his aged, ravaged cheeks,
He lies entombed in his own private hell.

Waiting to be taken, for his transcendence to the next realm,
He replays in his feeble mind the years of long ago,
Memories of births and deaths and laughs and sadness,
He has experienced now all that he has to know.

And so he bids a heart-felt goodbye to all that he has loved,
A precious lingering moment of contentment does overcome,

Then he closes his weary eyes, peaceful, oh so peaceful,
Waiting for the imminent eternal darkness, to succumb.

No more hurt or hate or pain,
He gasps one last long breath into his lungs,
Then blackness, soon to be something new, not old,
Fleeing mortality, he fades into the tunnel of life,
Intent upon a new destination,
Smiling, free, he is seeing the beauty after life that was long ago foretold.

Sharon Cameron

MOTHER NATURE

Beautiful roses by the door,
Bees and butterflies by the score,
The sun to brighten up the day,
The moon at night, to show the way.

This world of ours could perfect be,
If we, and others would agree,
We could make this a better place,
Leaving alone 'The Outer Space.'

There is a cure for all our ills,
Without the drugs, without the pills,
So let the cares o' battle cease,
And let the whole world live in Peace,

God's greatest gift, quite surely so,
Is mother nature here below,
The sun, the moon and stars above,
Are all a part of God's great love.

Jimmy Sinclair

SCARS OF MY HEART

Amid the daily emotions
lie the scars of my heart
life is the highest commodity
when loved ones are torn apart.

From mother's breast to rocking chair
when raging war enters our lives
men go in search of battlefields
as bees swarm from the hive.

Courageous actions are never ignored
medals won with loudening cheer
but only sadness for the mother
waiting for her son to reappear.

We know they fight for a reason
for this conflict to come to an end
but when all our sons are in Heaven
who then are we going to send?

James Shattock

SHORTBREAD STREET

Old maids swarm from narrow lanes
Bearded ladies with varicose veins
Clutch shopping bags bursting at the seams
With outsize knickers and custard creams.

The daily shopping ritual completed
They grudgingly pay their money
And are seated . . .
On the bus to shortbread street.

The bitterness of bygone youth
Consumes these women like a rotten tooth
Gossip, resentment and bunioned feet
Adorn the bus to shortbread street.

Straight white faces moan and complain
Of how the world is not the same
'That wouldn't happen in my day'
Is all you'll hear these Calvinists say
On the bus to shortbread street.

A stranger's face is an unwelcome sight
As the bus swings violently to the right
Der Fuhrer's in the driver's seat
On the bus to shortbread street.

David J Sime

WOMAN

She perceives with certainty
Her mind undeterred
Confidently speaking out
For her creed,
While sure of the direction
She moves toward
There is no need for doubt

As the millennium approaches,
Woman is no longer
Subservient, for
Being equal in status
She has clarity of vision.
Woman finds new courage
And is resolute
Therefore must be regarded
With respect

Irene Gunnion

A POINT OF VIEW

See the stars, trapped in the night,
those tiny beacons of twinkling light,
See the moon, white and round,
orbiting the earth not making a sound,
See the clouds, floating on high,
carrying water across our great sky,
See the waves in constant motion,
racing to cross that mighty big ocean,
See in the harbour, something afloat,
perhaps some driftwood even a small boat,
See the bushes and the trees,
toing and froing in the light breeze,
See the wall, straight and tall,
warding off intruders who call,
See down the pathway a shadowy fox,
no I'm mistaken, just peculiar shaped rocks,
See in the garden, the plants of June,
waiting for morning to spring into bloom,
See through the window on the settee,
that person looking back that person is me.

David White

CANIS LUPUS

The darkest night I ever saw,
Had a starless, moonless sky,
'Twas then I met a gypsy man,
With midnight in his eyes.

I gave to him my heart and soul,
Though he could not be true,
With blood so wild and spirit free,
My candle flame burned blue.

As dawns and dusks passed by and by,
The love I gave was taken,
I gave it freely though I knew,
That I would be forsaken.

Too soon the moon was bright and full;
He gazed with loving look,
The night herself called out to him,
To keep company with her wolves.

I plead with night to set him free,
As day makes way for gloaming,
I wish to be wherever he,
And his gypsy heart are roaming.

Alex Draven

CRETINS' REPOSE

Once upon a pillow
Somebody set their head
Dismembered body
Is blood red?

Wide open spaces
Never ending day
Far off horizon
Where does the crow fly?

Rolling stones
Desert sands
Raging rivers
Far away lands.

Tribes of faceless beings
Like lemmings before they leap
Is this a living nightmare?
Are we really fast asleep?

Margareth

DOLLY'S GRANNY

I remember dolly.
I found her in a skip.
She only had one eye
and some dogs had chewed off her lips

Abandoned in a bin.
She was abandoned in the dirt
So I took dolly home
And granny said I couldn't keep her.

But I sneaked her in my room
And I kept her there for some time
And when I took dolly out
Granny just thought she was mine.

Yet all my friends were jealous
And all my friends were sore
Cos now I had a dolly to love
They thought I didn't like them anymore.

But dolly she was my best friend
And they would never understand
Cos no one ever threw them in the skip
They had mums to love not grans.

Lisa O'Donnell

A SEDUCTION

We called it the silver screen, though really
It was shades of grey.

Shadows lived within its celluloid cells,
Coming forth, like the weekend gods they were,
To assume gigantic proportions
Before us.

Dancing, weeping, loving, deceiving
Their way through smoke towards us,
As we, the little people,
Clutched red velour
And choked on popcorn.

Harlow, Dietrich, Garbo, Bacall:
Talking tragedies to each little island
With a Saturday afternoon to spare
In the company of strangers.
The children, the couples, the drunks
(Who frankly didn't give a damn)
And perhaps in every few rows,
One like me.

O sacred screen of silver shades!
O festering flea-pit of fantasies!

There, my dreams had form and fuel;
There, my heart was rich with escape;
There, my world seduced -
With a whistle.

Julie Rothnie

RED SUN

Red sun . . . Shining above the rooftops
Embracing a world globally in grief
For *Children; Scotland's Flowers*
Now lying cold in tears of disbelief . . .

Red sun . . . break through on parents grieving
Embrace them in your circling arms of *Love*
Comfort them in their hours of disbelieving
Shelter them 'neath your rays and give them hope.

Red sun . . . symbol of God's eternal fire
shining through your fiery flames just now
Bursting through the clouds of dark despair
Shedding light and hope and brightness
On those shattered dreams of parents everywhere . . .

Margaret O'Donoghue

MY DAD

I need some inspiration
All mine seems to have gone
He gave me strong feelings
Whether good or bad
He gave me humour so that I could laugh
He gave me anger and frustration
That made me write like mad
But now he's gone
The anger and the laughter too
Thank you for being my Dad
I Love You

Justina Braine

THE VISIT

Frail fingers
fret and twitch the rug
- marked *Ward 9 Men* -
Nurse folds about your chair.

Incredulous
I watch the mindless movement
          of those hands -
age stained now
yet strangely soft and childlike.

Are they the hands
that plucked my innocence
made me wise?

I reach out
and clasp your fingers;
you gaze at me
through me
past me -
my grief is tangible
to all but you.

Nurse tells me
you are happy in your world;
it is only I
who rages
at the nothingness in your soul.

I urge you to feel life again -
pain
anger
passion;
instead

you smile -
benign
serene
so bloody indifferent.

Kitty Pawson

THE LIGHT, AFTER DARK, AFTER TIME

The sun it was shining
But it could not shine on me
The sun it was beaming
But it, I could not see
A dark cloud had descended
Obscuring all around
A loved one lost forever
On a journey Heaven bound.

Life it feels so empty
So dismal and so vain
Nothing seems to ease the heartache
The anger or the pain.
A dark cloud has descended
Obscuring all around
Everything is darkness
Relief cannot be found.

Time goes on and passes by
Can't forget, don't want to try
The pain is eased, the heart grows strong
Again I hear the birds in song
The sun, it is shining
And it shines on me
The sun it is beaming
And at last I see.

James Binnie

OIL RIG THOUGHT TANK

I smoke far too much
I should take more air,
my life revolves around a monstrous mish mash
of metal and moans,
three weeks away
three weeks of not wanting to be away
three weeks at home and three weeks of thinking about three
weeks away,
and so, on and on it goes, like another world revolving and rotting away . . .

Ian Ferguson

KIRKMICHAEL BOY'S LAMENT

Where are we goin' to ? What's the use,
They give us crap, and dog's abuse.
We're the scum, never number 1
So why bother a France what we have done!
We get the blame and suffer the shame,
'Kirkmichael boys' they're always the same!'
What do they know of our feelings deep.
Have they given a thought of what makes us leap?
A game o' fitba aroon at the shops,
Been goin' on for years, and never stops
So why do you all give us Hell,
When in your youth you did the same as well?
Think back on the days when you were young,
The things you did, the songs you sung,
Are we all so different from you?
Supporting the green, supporting the blue.
Think on it, think on it, think on it strong,
Adults are always right, youths forever wrong.

Kate Brown

VAMPYRE IN A SCOTTISH WOOD

In a frozen wood
the children of the night
were hunting
in a red mist
they came seeking sustenance
from your veins

on your breasts
a river of blood
the feeding frenzy of desire
a crimson pulse throbbing
a surge of power
in the red heat

in his filthy way
he did love you
a strange tenderness he felt
powders crumbling
Travelling at speed through the night

He offered you
power and knowledge
all wonders and delight
subtleties of feeling and sensation
freedom from growth and decay
the organic flux of things
the terrible in and out of it all

it was not true when they said
that he could not love
for he adored you
you were his crimson flower his beloved

J Roney

DECEMBER

Darkest December
Nothing
Exists at all
Except this view:
Ruberslaw a sweating
Steaming volcano
A reflex action
In memory of its past
The primordial genesis
Dinosaurs lurching
Falling
To sleep, forever.
In the sliver of
A snow-blind eye
Stands and stumbles
The Roman Empire
Trimontium a twisting
Triple gyroscope
Measuring every perspective
Along Deere Street
Ashkirk and Selkirk masts
A biopsy of a wider
Narrowed
Contemporary globe.
Soon be Christmas Day.
Another awakening.

Julian Colton

CIRCUMSTANTIAL EVIDENCE

He lays his head down
Among false hopes and faded dreams
Each night upon the park bench
Pulling up last week's newspapers
To diminish the reality of a finite
World. A bottle of liquid death
Lies almost empty at his feet.

His past lies latent stuffed inside
An old duffel bag
Memories and mental scars
Fight for pride and place in a meths
Sodden Brain

Twenty to sixty he's in there
Somewhere. A veteran of circumstance
Some call a tramp
A nomad of choosing. Familiar to
No one but part of us all.
For his aversion to sobriety the price has been paid.

He dreams of a future that has
Been dragged from the past
Plying for life while knocking
On death's door
Lifting the bottle he takes a last swig.

Joe McKinsley

VIRGIN SOUL?

The covert pervert
Peers and prys.
The overt voyeur
Lost, on unknown shores,
Laughs and sighs.
The virgin soul
In innocence becries
The pleasure of the pure.

Mad mystical mind mutations
Mimic mirth,
Murmur memories.
Gargantuan greed gleams
Global girth
As gruesome gentle men
Gorge on gentle Gods.
The virgin soul
In avarice condemns
The pleasures of the pure.

Succulent souls
Seep such septic sorrows.
Perfection awaits.
If only we had today
The dream of tomorrow.
The virgin soul
In time forgives
The pleasures of the pure.

Aka Jazz

BATTLE NONE

Reminisce
Loneliness
Try to hide
False side
Has been done
Damaged one
Delusion
End solution

Emptiness
Powerless
Weep inside
Foolish pride
Battle none
Remorse some
Conclusion
Institution

Helen Bain

HAMISH

Still just the same, after seventeen years, of searching,
and struggling, trying to remember, the warmth of your smile,
the love in your eyes.
No more desperate searching, for comforting memories.
You are here, I can touch you, yet you seem unaware,
of the pain you have caused, by your obvious absence.
Let me savour forever, this longed for reunion,
Happy and carefree, rejecting distractions, which suddenly
seem so ominously threatening.
It is cold and I shiver, please don't turn away, from my eyes
which are anguished, reluctantly opening, to the reality
of death, forgotten in a dream.

Catherine McCallum

HAPPINESS IS . . .

On a snowy winter evening,
The one thing I desire,
Is to sit inside with you, my dear.
My glowing, golden fire

When a hard day's work is over,
I walk quickly to the door,
You welcome me with open arms
And warm me to the core

You symbolise my nation
So strong and fresh and pure
And for any ailment I may have
You are my only cure

I'll keep with you all my life
And you will keep your watch
For you're an ever faithful friend
My trusty glass of Scotch

Greta Hughson

THE CATS HAVE WON IT

04.42 In bed. Lying
Without sleeping.

The night's breath brings a
Scream to my window.

Tomorrow I may read of another victim
Closer to home this time
Even be compelled to phone-in *Crimewatch*.

Perhaps it was a tyre-screech
Or cats fighting, mating, or both
Even all three.

Yes. As I turn over and curl
Into warmth and dreams I
Keep my eyes tightly shut.
The cats have won it.

Mark Fleming

'HE' WILL FLY

A rusty chilling light so round,
Lays colour on the darkened ground.

A cry disturbs the peaceful sleep,
Of happy children in comfort deep.

A frozen sea reflects a glaze,
Of cheerful lights in homes, ablaze.

The hills afar are barely seen,
Yet there's a peep from young eyes keen.

Swooping past the ground, so low,
Over the frozen sea below.

Is the joy the bairns await
And rise to feel the magic, late.

A box reveals a gift untold
To light the eyes of youth, till old.

A piercing yellow floods the sky,
Then a year will pass till 'He' will fly.

Karen Laird

OLD MR GRIEVE

Old Mr Grieve lives on the top floor
Nobody knows if he lives there anymore
Two world wars have passed through his eyes
But he still doesn't understand disco and rave

He'll talk to you all day, whilst you're in a hurry
On your way to work the pub or for a curry
You'll try to avoid him if you possibly can
Denying the passing of stories and pain

You really feel guilty for passing him by
But your life's just beginning and his is running dry
You wonder what life is like in a top story cage
Probably familiar, love, hope, anger and rage

You know that his life is empty and spartan
Fridge full of streaky, eggs and milk carton
You know that his home is furnished with air
His bank account healthy for passage to heirs

You know of his stories you've heard them before
You know he is independent down to the core
He used to help out in the back green
He leaves it to me now, younger and mean.

I feel I know nothing of the man
A family unseen, wife, brother, gran?
What mysteries of life does he hold in his head?
Would he tell me if I asked him, or put me to bed?

I feel that he holds the key to my life
If I could find the lock then I'd tell my wife
Old Mr Grieve lives on the top floor
Nobody knows if he lives there anymore

Do we care in a world full of crime?
Will we go up and see him, or leave it 'til next time?

David Love

64

BOB AND RAB AND I

Bob was my friendly mate for a year,
A good and trusty pal to be sure.
His life of eighteen years on earth
Began some time before my birth.
My elder, therefore, Bob was indeed
And I tried to tend his every need
Each morning at six I gave him Oats,
Turnips, and fodder in ample lots.
Bob was a horse it may be gathered
A Clydesdale horse quite old and withered
Yoked to a cart in farmyard or field
To threatening shouts Bob would not yield
His legs seemed to have given up hope,
He had but two speeds dead slow and stop.
That is how he was my very good friend
He did not work me hard you understand

Rab also was my pal, and human
He worked with Bob and I quite often
To match Bob plodding locomotion
Rab and I sought for mild distraction
While Bob was standing full-stop and still,
Which he quickly did with no ill will,
If we rubbed one itchy old hind leg
We laughed at Bob lifting the withered peg
So each of us stroked a nether shank -
The old boy quivered along the flank.
Then carefully eased against the cart
And promptly sat on the hind most part.
He looked like a dog about to beg
Camouflaged as a wily old nag
I swear that he knew and the reason why
He had put one over Rab and I!

Sandy Murdock

SHEEP IN MY GARDEN

You're in my garden again
I see you from my window
You catch sight of me
And hold my gaze
As I look into your pale eyes
I wonder what thoughts you have
As you graze and chew
      Graze and chew
The monotony of your life
Broken only by the seasons
And what of that moment of
      separation
When that which you bore
Goes far from you
Do you imagine that you
Will endure for ever?

Brenda Finegan

YOU WILL NEVER BE

I never seen your picture on the screen
She said it would be easier for me,
You're only nothing, a blob just now
What the hell does she know the cow!

You're still a living part of me,
I created you, you'll still never be,
I will think of you always, when it's over
I know my regrets, will never end.

What would happen if you be?
A boy or a girl, I cry, never will see,
I will bear the pain and emptiness,
Killing is a sin, nothing less.

Diane Rafferty

66

A TRUE FRIEND

Dear convalescing Canon Mackay
Me thinks you've a hot line with the man in the sky
Living proof the miracles there
For those who doubt, do not despair
Triple bypass and what is more
A new grandson to love and adore
A lovely man with a lovely wife
With God's grace an extended life
Give time time, our meetings say
When someone is healing it's the only way
It's hard to play the waiting game
If it's any solace we're all the same
With the help from Rena your loving wife
All too precious, as is life . . .

Jean Tennent Mitchell

LET THERE BE PEACE

There will be peace one day.
Upon this Earth of ours.
When men realise they
Have got too clever with
Atom bombs and war,
It only takes one demented soul
To blow us all to bits,
Sadam Hussain is still about,
He's a very misguided son.
He kills, burns and maims his People
Is it just purely for fun?
He set fire to lots of oil wells
He's not set on conservation
When men like him have finished
The World will not be fit to live on.

E C Williams

ME AND THE MOON

Very cold . . . again . . .
Very quiet
Without you . . .
very sad
Not to hear your gentle voice
Telling me what I already know . . .
Me and the moon . . . Miss you . . .
We could share the
Pink and orange mornings that
Burst, explode, spill and
Overflow all over me and
My world without you . . .
It makes the tinsel sparkle
Fascinating patterns on the sitting room ceiling . . .
Everything outside is covered white
And glows red from the
Most perfect sunrises . . .
The ice covered world
Twinkles hope like your eyes always did . . .
But the dark yet equally bright nights
Are the best times of all . . .
Me and the moon
Stand alone for hours
Sad, still solitary
Statues in life's madness . . .
But quiet moments are not quite the same
Without you
Me and the moon . . . Miss you

Netta Irvine

SONG OF SHOPPING PARADES
(To the Kingdom Centre)

and as a green gunge sea slops,
tar clear, broths up and blistered
ogre whale, who gawks, a shop
scene seems to slice by the boil,

blond lick
boy, unclipped, no
harness, space guns striding,
canters like a horny bee, cool
in black,

on the path of the straight,
a few more lines to iron,
starch man, uniform blue, marching
on the path, of the straight
seams, utensils, dusters, gleaming
from floor, not face, sombre is safe,
on the path of the straight
a few more lines to iron,

'bastard!' he flutters, cans leave cart,
playgrounds without jibes,
                        space boy smarts,
breezed-by breath sincere
with o.a.p. fear
like a deep
light gone dark,

reaching hands meet,
a generation connection,
just one dissipating random

as jostling plankton, sunday scraps, anticipate storms

Paul Clyne

WINTER TIME

Winter time can be such fun
How lovely to see the winter sun
The holly with its berries red
A woolly hat upon your head

The snow it falls down from the sky
All white and fluffy on the ground does lie
The children they come out to play
They see the snow and shout 'hooray'

They pull their sledges up the hill
They slide back down oh what a thrill
The sound of laughter brings great joy
A mother hugs her little boy

A snowman he stands firmly in place
A cheeky grin upon his face
A top hat's on his head held high
He smiles to everyone passing by

The icicles from the trees do fall
They're smooth and icy slim and tall
To sit around a warm log fire
What more could anyone desire?

Janet McBride

MYTHOLOGICAL TALES

Dragons
Imps
Long coat tailed wizards
Casting spells with lizard tails
And black shelled snails
Trying to capture banshee wails
All are figments of Imaginative Mythological Tales!

Hocus Pocus!
Alakazam!
People visiting the old wise man
Buying charms, cures and magical lures
Crocodile living in dirty sewers
Casting spells
Throwing pennies in wishing wells
Old wives' tales
All are parts of Imaginative Mythological Tales!

Shaun Foley (12)

REJECTION

Quarter past eight on the dot heard
postman's footsteps coming up path.
Popped letter through letterbox flap.
Heart uplifted could it be
Goodness! Postmark publishing company.

Great excitement, hand trembling
read letter soul went down
rejecting poem gave frown.
Although high standard 'How can that be?'
If it was all that good you would have published
for world to see.

Pen to paper wrote hastily,
dear editor of yours truly.
Please give me another chance without having
to go on bended knee.
I've been quoted as another famous poet
won't give up easily.
Do you really want rivals, 'Discover me!'

Dawn Constable

FORTUNES

Walking down the Vennel one day
I saw a gypsy look my way
She spoke to me and told me my name
I asked her how she knew
She replied
I am old and wise
And I have looked in your eyes

Tell me more I cried
As you are old and wise
She shied away from me and said
You must cross my palm with silver
And silver did cross her palm

She told me of two little children
One fair, one dark
A life of happiness and calm
That one day I shall have all I wished for

She wandered on up the Vennel
To tell another fortune
Another fortune she would tell
For a piece of silver.

C McCallie

THE NEIGHBOUR

Yesterday, mending your creels,
Today, gone to the deep.
'Your neighbour drowned!' they said,
But I could not take it in;
I had seen you this morning
In your yellow oilskins.
A freak wave, they surmise -
But the sea was not rough!

Heaven help the kin, and widow;
I have stood in her shoes,
I know how she feels;
But I cannot share her grief.
Work and time, I know,
Will ease the pain and heartache;
Because grief exhausts itself,
Or it exhausts the sufferer.

T M Minty

I WANT TO

I want to feel your body,
I want to share your pain,
I want to hold your hand once more in the rain,
I want to taste your kiss,
I want to call your name.

Because ever since we met I've never been the same.
When you call me on the phone the joy I can't explain,
When I see you in the flesh my body feels so tame.

So I want to feel your body,
    I want to share your pain,
    I want to hear your heart beat next to mine,
    I want to taste your kiss,
    I want to call you mine.

Because ever since we met I've never been the same
And so I want to ask will I see you again.

So can I feel your body?
    Can I share your pain?
    And can I hold your hand forever in the rain?

R W D McGough

THE BERWICKSHIRE LADIES' OPEN

The Berwickshire ladies' open race
A point to point with lots of pace
The Snowden entry, that is theirs!
Carrying our blessings, hopes and prayers

Seven runners, a very good field with dash
Dominated by Nicola, Blue with White sash
The favourite in the field, it lacked elation
Ridden by Valerie, called 'Hello Sensation'

The leader turned out to be 'Amber Payne'
It could have done with a little less rain
Our heroine was riding, trained to a turn
The jumps were easy for 'Rushing Burn'

Nicola was going from strength to strength
At each of the jumps she gained a length
One could see it was Nicola's turn
To win the race with 'Rushing Burn'

Ten lengths and a distance was the measure
The memory of which we shall always treasure
The reception they got was good to hear
Congratulations to all and many a cheer

The excitement and emotion of winning the race
Was equalled by the sight of the sisters' embrace
Nicola may not have won a race before
But we can see she'll win many more.

Andrew Spence

CANARY WHARF

A nameless bundle lies in wait,
Hidden well.
Time tick-tocks and plans our fate,
Living hell.
Warning call. An afterthought?
Cold and callous.
Chance to learn what they've been taught,
Murder. Malice.
In the name of peace, destructive token.
They will sing
For the cause but promise broken.
Human thing.
Dog eat dog, man kill man.
Cold, hard fact.
No other way? No other plan?
Coward's act.

Les Jaffray

REFLECTIONS

Let's wander in the lonely glen,
And think on days lang since gane.
The 'Soochin win' fae roon the ben
Like whispering echoes in a dream.

The empty hoose up on the brae
Thro time has 'withered' winter's storm
Deserted noo for mony a day.
An open door stan's a forlorn.

Tho' spring is wi' us once again.
'Time' is 'Ageless' in the hills.
Let's mak' oor wye hame by the burn
Keepin' thochts an' memories tae oorsels'.

S Winchester

THE HAGGIS

What's this doon here on my plate
It's the wee Scotch Haggis that's met its fate
It's found in the Heilans among heather and peat
And digs doon in the grun wi' its short stumpy feet
It has a fur coat to keep it warm
Si it can run aboot a winter storm.
To catch a Haggis is quite an art
for those wee creatures come oot in the dark.
It's a delicacy we have once a year
That's why a staun and stare . . .
in front of you aw here! Before I cut.
As I draw my knife from its pouch
I thought the wee thing may say ouch!
I am even glad to tell I thought it might even yell.
As the knife is drawn through and through
Wi' all the goodness coming to you.
Bulging oot comes aw the meet
Now I can say we're in for a treat.
As it's dished oot here on your plate
Let's have a thought before it's ate.
For these wee creatures Heilan born
Run oot in many a winter storm.
For they've been spied many a night
Long may they give us this delight!

James McDermid

THE ABERDABBY SOCIAL CLUB

There's a place called Aberdabby, to the west of Inverclabby,
With a little social club just outside town,
Where the local folk all meet, and sit drinking whisky neat,
As the bingo-caller shouts 'Eyes in! Look down!'

Now the Aberdabby Club, has become the social hub,
For the characters who live around the place,
Fat or thin, or large or small, let us go and pay a call,
On these curious members of the human race.

There's the blacksmith, Dopey Dan, who's a giant of a man,
He can shoe a Clydesdale horse in just a trice,
You may think that's pretty slick, but the reason he's so quick,
Is the horse is upside down, clamped in his vice.

The local shepherd Pat Macolley, who is fat and very jolly,
Owns a cross-eyed shaggy sheep dog known as Sam,
He said 'Not me you stupid tyke.' As he was butted o'er a dyke,
By the dog who had mistook him for a ram.

Now the postman Skinny Lees, who's six-foot with knobbly knees,
Was a bachelor who said 'All women I'll out-fox.'
But while delivering the mail, to the spinster Isa Wale,
She caught and pulled him through her letter-box.

The local baker Dirty Del, and his daughter Big Estelle,
Insist their hygiene standard's very high,
When confronted by a mob, Big Estelle was heard to sob,
'That's a currant in your doughnut, not a fly.'

So here ends this little ditty, and we trust you found it witty,
Of Aberdabby and its funny ways,
We hope a postcard you will send, for we sincerely recommend,
That you go there next year for your holidays.

Andrew Allan

VINCIT AMOR PATRIA

The smell of the shortbread wafted by, a bat retreated to the eaves, and I
Looked out on deer grazing in our grounds.
If this is Scotland, give me more,
Its beauty is endless - of that I'm sure,
But do I belong here, I ask myself, do I belong?
I secretly hope that in my ancestral past there is a drop of Scottish blood,
But alas, computer records show Saxon origin from a gentle family.

'Love conquers all in our homeland,' is the family motto,
The meaning I am glad to know,
As over the border I now live,
and it is with me wherever I go.
No animosity from my distinguished name will taint the soil of Scotland.
Does that mean I could claim the right to belong?

Three gold stags and a deer's head are my coat of arms and crest,
Emblems fit for any Scottish guest.
Do these symbols of the Highlands,
Signify that my land is not so different?
If the stag can roam and feel at home, surely the same applies to me.
I stand before you my friends and let you be my jury,
Put aside historical prejudice and you won't enact my fury.

Vincit amor patria
'Love conquers all in our homeland' and home to me is here,
The land just happens to be in Scotland, a land I hold most dear.
But do I belong here, I ask myself,
Do I belong?

C Whittaker

THE SCATTERING

For my father and your father
Both mine and your forefathers
This land was home;
Both heart and hearth,
Both blood and stone.
From the cradle to the grave
This Matriarchal womb
Encapsulated the community
Binding and tethering
Bonding love and loam.

And then that great broom called fate
Would hundreds sweep to clear the slate
Of the land and the people'd tread
Both near and far,
Those alive. More dead.
Whether abroad or to the worms,
The mother's burden spread
Out with the community
As adolescents leaving home
These mothers' children in search of bread.

Now that umbilical cord got broken
And the bright young sparks that the land had woken
When grown drifted away
- A necessity of a Nemesis
Both with happiness and a gravity
From the cradle to the cities
While the country life decayed -
Through their unsuspecting complicity
Of its ability to sustain.

Alan Clark

FUN FAIR

Only 4 weeks to go and then here it will be
saving my pocket money, you need lots you see
Oh the thought of it so great, so excited I just can't wait
To get ready and go through the park gate

It's the Fun Fair of course with all its bright lights
To see it in all it's splendour, such delights
You can't see a clearing for what seems like miles
The rides and stalls all colours and different styles

We wait a whole year for it to appear
Paying money to be filled with fear
It makes no difference we enjoy it so much
Our knuckles going white with our tight clutch

The Big Wheel gives your tummy gip
And then the Waltzers make you flip
Round and round we go so fast
Always saying this time is the last

The hall of mirrors makes us look strange
Tall, fat and small each one makes us change
The Dodgems are good for a bash
Deliberately driving with aim to crash

Then there's queuing up for something to eat
Candyfloss you just can't beat
Burger and chips with their smell in the air
Making our mouth water, it's so hard to bear

As night-time descends there's a chill in the air
But we have had a great time that's the fun of the fair
Out of the gate, for home we are bound
And in our minds the thoughts of the night will be found

Lorna Fleming

WILL

It was 1918
We gleaned from rubbish dumps
Iron cooking pots
To be made into shrapnel,
And gathered sphagnum moss
To dress the soldiers' wounds.
Our oldest brother,
The gentlest of the boys,
Was fighting the war
To finish wars.

It was 1918
Outside father was sowing seeds
To reap in the autumn,
When Will came home on leave
Wearing his Gordons' kilt
And scattered bullets
Over the stone floor.

It was 1918
Father was in the harvest field
When a wire came.
Kneeling on the ground
He read that Will was wounded.

It was 1918
And Armistice was
Just over a month away.
Mother and Ann went down
To Bangour Hospital to see Will.
His shoulder shattered,
He was unfit to garner
His inheritance of the farm.

Lorna Riddoch

THIS LONELY CELL

Sitting in this lonely cell,
Depression, dampness, and the smell,
I've been in prison most of my life,
Parted from my loyal wife,
She's had it all to do alone,
Raising kids without a moan,
All because I've been a skunk,
Thieving, mugging to buy my junk,
Breaking hearts along the way
The costly price I've had to pay
Another stretch I'm doing inside,
A broken man who's lost his pride.
On my knees I try to pray,
But my head's so scrambled I begin to stray,
To thoughts about my life in hell,
Sitting in this lonely cell.

Kenneth Meiklejohn

IF

If my fingers cannot touch your skin
Let them forever idle be
If my eyes are forbidden -
To search your depths
Be it only darkness that they see
If my voice cannot cry out your name
Then let it be struck dumb
If my body lies naked and alone
Let it be forever numb
If I heard the words I love you
But they were just a lie
Then let my heart stop beating
And slowly let me die.

Heather Johnson

WHO CARES?

How little I do and how much I care.
The balance is never entirely fair.
I'd like to try but how to make
My effort, with so much at stake.
Unfitted for a mammoth task
Is there some way, I sometimes ask.
Is opportunity there to see
Or does it quietly bypass me?
Success would mean if I could say,
'There's one heart happier today.'
It would not be too long before
The balance tipped a little more.
I know it's beckoning somewhere
There's much to do for those who care.

M F Morrow

SILVER MOON

O, silver moon, silver moon
What secrets do you hold?
Shrouded by a cloudy veil
Your beauty to unfold,
and as the night draws slowly on
a chillness in the air
a crisp white frost upon the ground
a stillness everywhere
but too soon your rival comes
with her soft warm glow
mother sun is waking up
as moon prepares to go.

Rosemarie Beverley

CHILDREN OF DUNBLANE

Now I look at children
I think of Dunblane
I think of their innocence
and think of their pain.

Now I look at children
I think of the relatives
and their heavy hearts
I think of the friends
and of the teachers
all left behind
their grief I cannot comprehend.

Rivers of sadness
flow from my eyes
I'm ashamed to say
I'm a human being
life seems so pointless
but in times of grief
we find an inner strength
we find the will
to carry on somehow.

Throughout the centuries
children have endured persecution
they're an easy target
they can't fight back
so it is the children
we must look to
for courage and strength.

There is a future
maybe not this year
or the year after
but it is there in the distance
far away from that evil evil man
he is where he can do no more harm.

For Gwen Mayor and her shiny buttons
a classroom in heaven
on earth a memory forever.

Susan Thomas

A BEAUTY OF ITS OWN

I witnessed nuclear holocaust
In a dream I had last night
It caused a state of wonderment
More sorrow than of fright
It happens in the future
Of that I'd fairly bet
It's not the sort of happening
That you're liable to forget
I saw the smoke ring rising
Quite close to where I stood
It blossomed out a hundred fold
I whispered 'Oh dear God'
I shouted to those closest
To get behind this wall
No sooner had I said this
When a blackout hit us all
I remember struggling to my feet
The worst was yet to come
I remember feeling dizzy
When the air began to hum
It wasn't really painful see
As we waited for the blast
We saw concentric circles come
Quite beautiful quite fast.

R Speirs

STOLEN LOVE - THE PARTING

The dawn is breaking
The sleepless night ends,
A new day is beginning
But not for me - I have lost you my friend.

Friend ! No - much more than a friend
If it were only friend
Why do I feel
My world
is at an end.

Yesterday - all my yesterdays
Were full of joy and love.
A meeting - sometimes by chance,
I walked on air
You were there!

And now, we say goodbye,
So many are the tears I've shed,
Your touch - the ecstasy - the joy
Is no more.
I wish that I were dead.

Christina Mailer

MY HAMELAND

Silver rivers white with foam
Blue mountains that I love to roam.
Lovely glens all wet with dew
Bonnie Scotland I love you.

Royal Stag with head held high
as proud as 'Charlie' in days gone by.
With heart so strong, so loyal and true
Bonnie Scotland I love you.

Emblem of Scotland thistle grand
I hold with pride within my hand
With stem of green and flower blue
Bonnie Scotland I love you.

Ye Banks and Braes of brown and green
The bonniest sight I've ever seen
Highlands, Islands, Lowlands too
Bonnie Scotland I love you.

Rod Hynds

STREET TRAFFIC

Cars, lorries, and buses,
Up and down every street,
With rear ends a' smoking,
Sound, cheeky beep beeps.

From Monday to Sunday,
Day and night of the week,
There's all kinds of traffic,
Not just on two feet.

Coming from all sides,
There's some take no heed,
Looked at from sidewalk,
It's a western stampede.

You see a bus coming,
It's one that you need,
Attempts to cross over,
Are feats to concede.

The hustle and bustle,
Hoards of people you meet,
Think sometimes I'd rather
Jump over the creek.

Katie Munro

POP

My grandfather was a special man.
His eyes crackled with kindness and mischief,
Their sea-greeness told stories of
Hard times,
Happy times,
Let's-get-up-to-mischief-times.
His lined face - weathered and
Furrowed with hard work and laughter,
Evoked memories of times long past,
His easy going lilt,
Was known and loved by everyone,
Cracking jokes,
With unknown folks,
Plotting pranks with all 'his cronies'.
His listening, caring, slightly-deaf ears,
Heard all they needed to,
Especially when 'Time gentlemen please!' was called,
Or when I needed to moan.
His big, soft, rough hands
Cradled me when I was a baby,
Picked me up when I skinned my knee,
Held me tight when I cried.

He was known as Todolo.

Patricia A J Masson

THE TYPICAL GLASWEGIAN GENT

His voice is lost in the vast throng
of people, all that is audible is
paper paper!

With monotonous gravel voice it goes
on and on, in his own Glasgow dialect.
When there is a few seconds pause, he
is serving a punter

He is nobody's fool is that little gent,
for he is a typical Glaswegian with
his sharp wit.

He is one of Glasgow's characters with a
simple philosophy to life, for he can
Charm the most surliness person
to come away from him, with hint
of a smile playing around their
mouth.

'No matter what the element he is
There at his pitch till his last
paper is sold!'
Long after you have passed him
his persistent drone is still
ringing in your ear!

No doubt he will be at
the selling, paper! Paper! His
voice will ring, tomorrow again!

'For he is the typical Glaswegian Gent!'

Esther Rehill

COULD SOMEBODY TELL ME

Could somebody tell my confused little mind
What life is about and why it's unkind,
We struggle and toil for the sake of survival
Where pleasures are few inner strength is so vital.
Corruption and crime are increasingly rife
Fear in our hearts, is this what we call life?
What do we see for the next generation?
Nothing but misery and great deprivation.
The good life exclusive to the rich and the greedy,
Hardly a thought for the poor and the needy.
The system has failed its proud nation's folk
Contempt for the government is rightfully spoke.
The future? Who knows it's anyone's guess
A miracle is needed to sort out the mess,
Could somebody tell my confused little mind
What life is about and why it's unkind.

Lynne Back

THE POEM

Here I sit poised ower the lines
My hied fair in a bustle
Scartin like a plooket hen
No worth a penny whustle

The watters lappin ower the bows
She's gien me the slip
The muse the fickle hussie
Has scuttled aff the ship

Goad! There's the latch, I'm sunk!
Doon'll come the ceiling crashin
There's a heap o'dishes ben the hoose
I said I'd dae the washin.

J McD

EXTRACT OF A LETTER

As I lie here, looking into the flame
Of a solitary burning candle
My mind drifts back, thro' the passage of time
To a twilight beach
Us two wrapped in one another's arms
Staring deep into the flickering light
Of another flame
The dying sun giving rise to our moon
Are you really so far away when you
burn so bright in my heart?
You are so alive in my mind
The memory of your touch and of every caress
Stirs flames deep inside
Taking me higher, deeper . . .
Come with me into the realms
of my fantasy.

Gillian Deas

THE BURNINGS

Let the sheep graze
On charred remains of a lifetime
Delved from barren soil, but cherished
Ashes of an age now raked for fresh beginnings
The people swept away under a carpet of seaweed
Unwanted and alien
Betrayed, but never beaten, undeterred
No stormy sea can staunch the flame awaiting to be fanned
From buried embers
Their spirit smoulders in the ashes of their heritage
Unbroken, unquenched, unrelenting
Endlessly enduring
Let the sheep graze.

Marie Bennet

IN THE LAW LIBRARY

Jurisprudence of Holland
lies on the shelves with
Basilica and *Delict* and just about everything.

Not this, nor that is ample
enough to win your case, sir.
Says who? All on past example; everything to know is there.

Books of lives and law lie
on the shelves, on the table.
Precedents, principles, let's justify:
surely *Law's* not just a fable?

We examine the *but ifs* and the according *tos*.
Killing's right if we can make a killing?
The bar if we win, bars if we lose.
Who wants a job that's just fulfilling?

Wooden tables, wigs, gowns of black,
'Surely that's vindicatio (in rem)?'
Latin lovers look back
to consecrated judges in memoriam.

Taking every case, every view to the letter.
Can't we see right or wrong for ourselves?
Or were people from the past much better?
Law books live and lie on the shelves.

J F Griffin

REACH FOR YOUR DREAM

Reach for your dream, reach for a star,
No matter how near, no matter how far.

Follow the path, though it may, not always be straight,
Keep following that dream, though the burden be great.

Don't turn aside, no matter what,
Keep right on and unravel the plot.

Don't get downhearted, don't get low,
Get right on up and follow the flow.

So reach for the star, that's just out of your grasp,
Reach out and touch it and in your fingers it clasp.

Your goal is in sight, though it may not always seem,
But it can be for you, if you follow your dream.

Robert Kerr

REFLECTIONS

I looked into the mirror today
An old man looked out at me
And when I grinned hesitantly
His response was clear to see
His mouth smiled - so too his eyes
His whole face was a story
Etched there was pride and joy
And also grief and glory
At first I saw resemblance
Who could that stranger be?
Then sudden recognition
That old man was really me!

Alan Nicholls

WHAT HAVE WE DONE

If only people would look around
To all the beauty that's to be found
The tree's the flowers the soft green grass
Will soon be a beauty of the past
The war's raged on and things destroyed
There's millions of starving girls and boys
The animals they've become less and less
Our great big world is such a mess
They spend our money on tanks and guns
We're even destroying our only sun
The air we breathe just isn't clean
Just what does all this really mean
If only people would understand
The fate of this world is in our hands
We cannot turn the clock hands back
What's happened in life is now a fact.

Yvonne Little

A MUCH NEEDED LANGUAGE

As Scots we boast heroic deeds, our battles and our fame
But if the truth be honest told we would hang our heads in shame
By English sword and lack of heart, we've let down every son
And adopted English culture, English ruling, English tongue.

To dwell on Bruce of days gone by, of Wallace and Rob Roy
It's a folly that we all must stop and fill our hearts with joy
Our aim must be to lift our hearts and seek a new yardstick,
And outlaw speaking English; teach our sons to speak Gaelic.

In brave heart many hearts were stirred, a passion was unleashed
But in reality it's just a film, so no lesson will it teach.
As the song denotes, rise up again and once more be a nation
And put Scottish Dukes and all they hold, South, in their proper station.

I hold no malice or bad intent against our English friends
'Twas in the past these deeds were done, please see what's my intent
We need the Gaelic to be free and once more be our own
Let's teach it in our schools and homes; let Scotland stand alone.

Sandy McTavish

CRAFTED

My dad had skills with materials,
his hands were rough but he could feel
the shape of the wood or the bend of the steel.
He worked on ships that graced the seas,
with a proud tradition of quality.

Each tradesman's craft he learned with time,
applied each when making all the fine
toys, and gifts that became mine.
Took me high upon strong shoulders,
guided me as I grew older.

Now he's small, bald and grey,
but still big in my eyes as every day
I've learned to understand his ways.
The craft of love that now I see
was what he used to mould me.

Eric Brown

CHILDREN

I don't show my true love for the children in case it shows too much,
Deep down they know it's there, but in life such things are as such.
When they cry your shoulder stretches as far as need be,
And angry days they declare, then its firm hand they shall see.
Two sides of a coin it seems, when they can comfort and be comforted,
Bringing past events to the future with them, laughter and tears and
                                        events to be interpreted.
From hindering to helping, the latter to the fore,
Sweet smelling bathed bodies, to some outdoor relished gore.
Timing it so you can't sit down, they know how to light your fuse,
And they're ganging up when one's chips are down, to catching them
                                        out with yet another ruse.
They stumble over life's obstacles that you swore you had never done,
In reality though, years previous, if you hadn't done them too, then you must
have at least done some.
When your babies in their turn, start looking after you,
All the love you held within for years, comes finally shining through.

M Murphy

THE LITTLE FROG

There was a time when all our dreams,
Would fit into a jar
A little frog; a piece of string;
A fish shaped like a star.

Those treasures we would wish at night,
Were wished for, fierce and strong,
Then there it was! A liquorice rope,
To last the whole day long.

But now the jar is empty.
Our dreams won't fill it up.
It lies in a basement cupboard,
Gath'ring memories of dust.

And underneath the darkened porch,
On a still, but rainy day,
You can see a lonesome, little frog,
Steal silently away.

Linda Walker

A GAP IN THE CLOUD

The grey sky of winter goes on forever,
Endless puffs of smoke ascend from the chimneys,
The little aeroplane circles around and around,
Waiting for a gap in the cloud.

On the ground the children play,
Wrapped up in hats and scarves and gloves,
Kicking leaves around and around,
And looking for a gap in the cloud.

In the office a young man looks
Out of the window; he sees no joy,
He stirs his coffee around and around,
While searching for a gap in the cloud.

An old lady sits on a bus
Clutching her shopping in carrier bags,
Memories in her head go around and around,
She hopes for a gap in the cloud.

A widower passes the park
For what he is searching he won't find,
He wants his wife pacing by his side,
But she had found a gap in the cloud.

Sarah A Brown

BITING THE HAND THAT FEEDS

Looking through life's material haze
The voice of reason whispers softly
Many a time there's been a craze
But never a one so costly

Man has waged war just for the glory
And slaughtered his brothers for profit
For thousands of years it's been the same story
Because no-one seems willing to stop it

Now our attention has turned on another
The very one, we should worship and nurse
We are slowly but surely killing our mother
Our friend that has never denied us

And if you ask them, the reason why?
They say it's in the name of progress
It's easy to see through this lie
From people who really don't care less

This is one war, we can never win
No soldier nor general would cherish
For what we are doing is truly a sin
As the earth and its children will *Perish*

Richard Allan

A BETTER WORLD

In these days of technology,
And multi-million corporation,
Why is there still poverty,
Homelessness and deprivation?

Are we going backwards,
In this forward civilisation?
Or is it just pure ignorance,
In this ever-increasing population?

We all try to make a better world,
Are we going to succeed?
How do we make hypocrites and bigots,
Sit up and take heed?

Make this world a better place,
Before it's all too late,
Kindness, tolerance, aid and solace,
Should be everybody's fate . . .

Laura Duncan

UNTITLED

Smokey and Misty, our feline friends
When you're both together the fun never ends,
You're so content, when we see you, you purr,
From head to tail I stroke your vibrating fur.

Windy or rainy, you're always around
You always make those pussycat sounds.
I wish I could keep you for a day,
or a week, but you'd be missed, for
you your owners would seek.

You're both identical, both are grey,
I speak to you both every other day
You're both superior,
You're the king of cats,
You ladder my tights, but I can live with that.

You two loving cats,
You make my day,
I ask for one thing, just don't go away.

Alison Bowie

IS ANYBODY OUT THERE?

Search silently, little friend, search well
There are millions, millions of stars to choose from
Burning in the blackness like a distant hell

Supposed wise men, scientists, have cast a spell
Initiating your mission to go like no other
Search silently, little friend, search well

In dark wastes, electronics within your cold shell
Will discover a planet where intelligence dwells
Burning in the blackness like a distant hell

What if, in ensuing eons, during which empires fell
No memories existed of your distant quest?
Search silently, little friend, search well

What sort of dilemma then, when you tell
That your search has finally found success?
Burning in the blackness like a distant hell

And if that intelligence attacks, will you tell?
Warn us, with a final, electronic yell?
Search silently, little friend, search well
Burning in the blackness like a distant hell

Anthony Dalziel

SCOTLAND

Scotland, your beauty, so special and rare,
Your mountains are rugged, your glens are so fair.
From highland, to lowland, east coast to west,
To a true Scotsman, you are simply the best.

Your national dress, the kilt and the sporran,
Makes all Scots proud, and glad they were born.
White heather for luck, and bag-pipes a calling,
They march down the street, the music enthralling.

With love reaching out, to the ends of the Earth,
The exiled, are drawn, to the land of their birth.
To Scotland, their birthplace, the dream of perfection,
To carry back with them, the love and affection.

Instilled in the heart, for as long as you live,
Pride in one's country, is what mothers give.
To children, the future, is life's precious dream,
The dream to be nurtured, is Scotland the brave.

Shirley Thompson

CHILDHOOD DAYS

'Eat that up,' 'Sit down,' 'Be good.'
'Wrap up warm,' 'Pull up your hood.'
Orders given every day,
to little ones upon their way.
Their learning days all filled with fun,
of stories, nursery rhymes and Mum.
Helping here, and caring there
time to laugh, and play and share.
Such precious days, so soon long gone,
enjoy them all, forget not one.
They soon grow up *my* mother said,
when I wished them both in bed.
But she was right, of that I know
they'll both leave me, and off they'll go
like I left her to do my 'thing'.
I wish them well to have their fling.
But not quite yet, we'll wait a while.
Their faces beaming with a smile,
they're only little now you see.
My two twins are only three!

Heidi M Sands

MOTHER DEAR

You don't have to tell me
I can see your heartache
It's so clear in your eyes
I've experienced the same
When someone really close dies
A pain that's like no other
Especially when it's for
Your own dear mother.

> Mother dear
> I'm sitting here
> I'm waiting by your side
> Mother dear
> I'm sitting here
> Waiting for the eternal tide

You'll pray, you'll wish, you'll hope.
But deep inside feel numb
Waiting for a peaceful end
For dear sweet mum
Remembering times
Of her love and care
And her last few pennies
She'd always share.

Time will pass
And the pain will ease
Things you could have said
You might even regret
But for your dear sweet mother
You'll never ever forget.

Jules Tindal

LOVE

Love is living all your life for someone you adore
Love is giving all that you have got to give, and more
Love is always being there, and always being kind
Love is taking hurtful things, and knowing not to mind
Love acts quite unselfishly, and love is never hard
Love is doing extra tasks, and seeking no reward
Love is being happy when your loved one's feeling glad
Love is understanding when your dearest one is sad
Love stays waiting patiently whenever things go wrong
Love looks on the bright side, and is never sad for long
Love is constant, kind and true, and love can never cease
Love brings solace to the mind, and to the heart brings peace
Love can conjure miracles in times when troubles fall
Love can move the mountains, is the strongest force of all
All these things are part of love, but it is manifest -
A loving heart will reap the joy of being truly blest

Jane Gilbert

UNTITLED

And there was a beautiful place
With no sign of life, and the sea crashing in
Where the violence of waves, is of no crime
A mark of nature's beauty, that touches the soul
With awesome chunks of a world once been
Now worn to luscious islands of green
In the night's grey mist, like warriors they stand
Stubbornness and gentleness, underwater hand in hand
Those great chunks of rock, many changes they've seen
But wondrous parts of nature, they've always been
Look away from this man-made world
'There's always a beautiful place'

Louise Park

THE CAT

He meanders in - a persona of reverential dignity.
Walks with intent to the fridge
And waits, patiently expectant, self assuredly
Then pounces as the bowl is filled.
Milky waves swell and sway as he laps.
Not yet satisfied, he sits stolidly and waits for more.
Once replenished his tongue caresses milky pearl drops
from his whiskers.
He stretches, slowly, his body taut
Then draws himself in, back arched, fur quilled.
His tail swishes purposefully as his emerald eyes
scan the room
Seeking solace, solitude in the sun
He finds it, and pads protectively on his pillow.
With rasping tongue he rakes and strokes his fur clean.
Yawning warmly, he curls himself up
And wallows in the glow of satiety.
Too sleepy, the purr dies whispering on his lips
And rumbles gently deep below.

Diane Cumming

BE THANKFUL FOR TODAY

Be thankful for the present - appreciate what you've got
Forget the days of long ago - be happy with your lot
And as you look around you and see how others fare
Be thankful for your comforts - be thankful for your care

Allow yourself a little dream - of happy younger days
Of hopes and plans you cherished as you wandered throu' life's maze
But never dwell - at length upon - those days now long since gone
Today is more important - for you - and everyone

Your friends, your home, your interests all mean so much. It's true
Living for the present will safely see you through.
And, 'What about the future?' People have been heard to say
But, why worry about tomorrow - tomorrow's another day.

So let us see those shoulders back and a smile upon your face
A feeling of well being as you tackle life's fast pace
Remember these few friendly words as you go on your way
Be thankful for the present - be thankful for today.

Sandy Reid

THE TRUE SENSE OF THE WORD

There's no logic in language, just warped ABC;
Only those of good standing a chairman may be!
Grammatical mischief has plagued us from old;
Our temperature's up 'cause we're down with the
cold!

What's the name of that bird which looks just like a
pigeon?
If the clue lies in like-sounds, I'll find it, with luck.
Now here's one with promise - it's surely a wigeon -
But I should have said dove; for a wigeon's a duck!
And what of that creature which twins with the
Tortoise?
Through my lists of like-spellings I avidly hurtle.
I knew it! I've found it! It must be a porpoise!
But no, that's a dolphin. The right one's a turtle.

When I look at the building of each English word
I see aimless noun-doodling and codes quite absurd
Not the fruit of some learned labours love
But random ciphers of a topsy-turtle dove.

David T Collins

105

FANTASY

When life closes in and I'm tempted to flee
From the crowds, just to be quite alone,
I have a bolt-hole which beckons to me -
A refuge, a place of my own.

This place has no limits, no boundaries to hold
Me inside; it's a wide open space
For my mind to fly free as a bird, uncontrolled.
It's a mystic, ephemeral place.

I can be whom I like or go where I please,
Do the things that I've never dared do,
With no inhibitions, no folk to appease,
No regrets, no missed chances to rue.

Here all my terrors I can allay,
Feel joy surge as my hopes soar on high;
The pipe-dreams which get me through each trying day
Find their wings as I reach to the sky.

When I'm alone I can take off the face
Which I keep for confronting the world.
Relinquish control in my own private place
With my held-in emotions unfurled.

If I like I can sink to the depths of despair,
Let self-pity rise over my head.
My bruised self-esteem can come under repair
As my traumas and doubts I can shed.

So I never need fear what life may have in store,
For I know that, should confidence slip,
I can go to the harbour of hope with my dreams
And cast off on my fantasy's ship.

B Adamson

CANADIAN DREAM

I dreamt we went to Canada,
To visit James and Kay.
They welcomed us with open arms
It really made our day.
We drove out to their spacious house
By the Miramichi river
We met their lovely family there
Our hearts were all aquiver
We saw the sights both old and new
We loved 'McDonald's Farm'
We clopped along by horse and cart
With style and old world charm
We visited 'Kings Landing'
And stepped right back in time
To see how people lived and worked
In eighteen-forty-nine
We took a trip to Niagara
The mighty falls to view
Cascading like frothy lace
Against a sky of blue
All too soon our time ran out
And we had to shed a tear
But I'll just have another dream
And visit them next year.

Betty Shanks

EYES OF A SOLDIER

Marching on to what lies ahead,
Afraid with paranoid eyes
Passing bodies lying dead
Some, screaming soul rending cries.

Rifle held loaded to kill;
Death knocking at the door
Darkest nights, silently still,
Crouching down on Earth's floor

Shocked, finding safety within a trench
Frozen, some soldiers just want to hide
Many, shooting down the enemy dead,
While brother British soldiers bled.

Looking around to what's been found,
Lost in wonder still being alive
In an instance of a second;
His life and bravery being beckoned.

A bomb drops to his feet, it does arrive.
Death is now near and promptly here
No way now for him to survive;
His haggard face full of fear

When he falls, fall he must;
His soul may triumph in the dust
He fought peace for kids and brothers freed
A kinder world, a cleaner breed

Norma Watherston

PAISLEY'S REALITY

Sub zero night, day is breaking
Prowling foxes, bins are raking
A muffled sound, the lid it opens
From the bin, a man has woken
Through frozen eyes, he looked at me
Shivers down my spine, this is reality.

Walking down the road, my step is quickened
Looking around, my stomach is sickened
What used to be, a prosperous street
Second hand shops, my eyes did meet
I wondered why, this should be
All businesses gone, this is reality.

People pass by you, with expressionless faces
Not the time of day, only quickened paces
No friendly smiles, or cheerful hellos
Sense the pressure, feel how it grows
No time for caring, from you or me
Why is this happening? This is reality.

Many things, have pathed this way
Feelings deep, we should have our say
Wages lower, the Thatcher years
Employee's conditions, it will end in tears
Children learn, from what they see
God help us all, Paisley's reality.

Sylvia White

THE LAW OF LOVE

I've come to write the law of love
I've been sent down from above
When it is all on paper and pen
It better never ever be broken

The punishment is so severely strict
You'd better choose the right one to pick
If you don't it's going to make you sick
You'll feel like a fool with a new trick

Age doesn't count to the mad hatter
Since when did size or shape matter
Young or old will tell you this
Hot or cold, greet love with a kiss

Take a look, a blink, and it's gone
Like the sun the law of love is shone
Say exactly what is going through your mind
And true love one day you're sure to find

Some say true love is to die together
Are they very stupid? Or very clever
Judge and try not the rules
Let them break them, only the fools.

John A McVey

FEAR

When I was sick I lay in fear
Was my death drawing near?
The whispers of the daily nurse
Seemed only to make things worse
The voices in my head spoke out
To me, they seemed to scream and shout
Were they calling me to come?
To God knows where!

I then looked back in all I've done
Mistakes and lessons are all in one
Have I learned to not look back
Going forward was my track.
But then I prayed and prayed to stay
Here on Earth for other days
To carry on the 'learning' scheme
So now of Heaven, I only *Dream.*

Moira Michie

UNTITLED

Memories become lost in the mists of time
Dreams of times abandoned for things more sublime
Ambitions fade in the light of day
Often we walk the path of life the wrong way
Have you ever felt you've done things wrong
Listened to wrong advice, sung the wrong song
Often thought life would be better
If you'd never written a wrong letter
Ever said the wrong thing to someone who cares
Regretted it later when they're not there
Said I love you and not really meant it
Wishing you could somehow repent it
We all have the chance to start anew
All the choice our thoughts to review
To start afresh with fresh thoughts
Forget all the zeros, all the noughts
To lead life as it's meant to be
Happy, kind, gay and carefree.
It's not so hard to mend our ways
Turn dull moments into bright days
A little kindness, a little thought
Happiness is the dividend you'll have bought.

A Stevens

THE WHALES

We once were free
Roamed waves and sea
Together

But man's cruel heart and selfish will
Causes him to hurt and kill
Forever

We now are few and getting less
For massacre and bloody mess
Destroys us all

But beasts shall one day seek revenge
No more upon a man depend
And they shall fall

Alyson Hunter

ABERDEEN CITY

Aberdeen is a beautiful city
Situated between the Dee and the Don
Aberdeen is the silver city
Has a lovely beach known for its golden sand

Aberdeen is the granite city
Union Street is a sight to be seen
Aberdeen is a Britain in Bloom City
Its record shows it's second to none

Aberdeen is the oil city
A city that filled our heart with pride
Aberdeen is a fast growing city
People visit our city from far and wide

M Emslie

MUM

There is a woman in my heart
　　　　Who left not long ago . . .
Although four thousand miles apart,
　　　　She's never far from home.
She cradled me when I was young,
　　　　And calmed my piercing cries . . .
Then lulled me into thoughtless sleep,
　　　　To where danger never lies.
She fed me when I was hungry,
　　　　And she smothered all my fears . . .
She took away the bitterness,
　　　　And wiped away my tears.
She taught me the laws of life,
　　　　Through good and bad times gone . . .
She showed me how to stand alone,
　　　　In this world I call my own.
She bore me as an infant,
　　　　And raised me as a child . . .
She gave me everything a man could want,
　　　　With her love and grace entwined.
And that's how I say,
　　　　And I'll let no other . . .
　　　　　　Ever take the place of my dear mother.

James Wilson McMenemy

THE SOLDIER

There was a lad who went to war
He served his country on far off shores,
With sweat and toil he laboured on
For country and freedom he fought their foes,
He saw his friends around him fall
And sorrow pierced him to the heart,
Although his God had made this call
It saddened him to have to part.
Now weak and tired by what he saw
He began to falter in his stride,
To him this was inhuman law
That ones so young had fought and died.
'Courage brother do not stumble,'
These words to his mind did recall
Remembering this made him feel humble,
Not knowing he too would give his all.
Though the war years now have gone
And peace now reigns within this land,
In memory these lads live on,
The soldiers of God's chosen band.

William H Watson

GLASGOW

The city of culture is no more
The honour passes on
It's back to auld claes and purritch
Bright fantasy has gone

Red sandstone buildings rise from the green
Mushrooms of grey scattered between
but lurking behind the glorious facade
Poverty, cruelty, bad and the mad

114

For most it's enough to live, eat and sleep
with thoughts that seldom run so deep
to appreciate the sights, the sound and art
of which the City of Culture was part

Big Issue is selling, instead of Voltaire
Wee wifies are invading elite Princes Square
The universal pub chorus, voices deep, and so rough
'We don't haud wi all a' that Arti Farti stuff!'

Ellen J Bruce

THE MAGIC LANTERN

Memories are pictures,
Pictures in the mind,
Each one carefully catalogued,
Of every type and kind,
Archived, not forgotten,
Brought forth upon recall,
To reproduce emotions,
Known to one and all,
Happy times, sadness too,
Each one has its place,
People long forgotten,
An unremembered face,
Children round the firelight,
Staring at a Christmas tree,
That cosy little bundle,
Upon its mummy's knee,
These things are all worth keeping,
Let none be left behind,
Cast by the magic lantern,
Showing pictures of the mind.

Andrew Quinn

A MAGNIFYING GLASS TO OUR MINDS

Looking at people's faces
Can you ever find traces,
Of happiness, sadness or
Even madness,
Can you see their inner thoughts,
Signs of distraught,
Just from the average person,
What are their intentions,
Are they deceptive,
Or are they respective,
Can you really tell by looking
At someone
What they've done,
Do we analyse?
Or let them pass us by . . .

Sonia Conway

ON THE ROAD TO INVERNESS

Oh stony strichen bloody mess
Man woman and child lay abreast
Its passage laden with blood and Highland dress
On the road to Inverness

The aftermath of Culloden had begun
To rid the Highlanders from their land
Language culture way of life
To be slaughtered by musket, sword and knife

Dirty grey clouds dreary wet and cold
Hanovarian soldiers brutality proud and bold
Leave behind their scars infested by their zest
Shattered prodigy on the road to Inverness

Richard A MacLean

THE RIVER

Trickling, rippling in the sunshine
Over stones, moss and mud.
Ever swelling, stronger, wider
As downward it flows.
Swirling, clinging, ever circling
Tall reeds and grasses.
Creatures splashing, dark eyes sparkling
Hurry, scurry - splash!
A silky-smooth deceptive calm
Abruptly shattered -
A sudden drop of torrents white
Where rainbows linger.
Here, salmon struggle helplessly
Currents to defeat.
Here, fishermen wait patiently
Rod and net in hand
Calmer waters tempt the oarsman
His skills to employ.
Urban mills, their waste expelling -
Murky waters flow.
Unsuspecting ducks and wildlife
Bounce and float along.
The smell of salt and shriek of gulls -
River joins the sea.

Irene Rose

WE'LL MEET AGAIN

I fell out with a lady
Who turned out to be your ex wife
I never knew then that
You would be part of my life

We seemed to get on fine
But I was seeing another man.
He turned out to be married
That's when our relationship began.

At first it was only sex
Then it got exciting
It was very strange
Then we began fighting

I found out I was expecting
You ran a mile
When our baby was born
You visited a while

He's eight years old now
You died when he was seven
We both still love you
We'll meet you again in heaven

C Florence

DAY TRIP

We save all year round our pennies with pride
For our yearly jaunt to the nearby seaside
We catch the train to take us away
To the golden beach with the horseshoe bay

There's mother and father and granny too
Sand-castles and swimming hundreds to do
We've brought along our new bucket and spade
And the high flying kite that grandpa had made

We'll have our picnic on a big tartan rug
Sandwiches and crisps lemonade from a jug
After for a treat an ice cream from the stand
And then on to watch the big brass band

We have to go home after the donkey ride
If we stay on the beach we'll get washed with the tide
We'll make our way home so happy that's clear
Where we'll quickly save up for another year.

Elizabeth McIntyre

TOBRUK THOUGHTS

As I walk the stony paths of life
In my constant search for peace
I see the tension all around
And pray that it would cease

It is a forlorn hope I know
For the state this world is in
It has taken us so many years
To concoct this pressure bin

Mankind has done a lot of good
But we have too many faults
To create a perfect peaceful world
Should be our foremost thoughts

The nations all stand divided
We're at each other's throats
There's people dying from hunger
And from the cold through lack of coats

As I gaze upon the stars at night
I cannot help but wonder
Is there a peaceful people there
Somewhere in that far yonder

J R Kemp

GONDOLA

My arm through yours, against the vaporetto rail,
we sail down the reflections of the Canal, with
Venetian Douglas Hurds; young Claudia Cardinales in
costly shoes, and hint
of peach cheeks.

The visitor's lips go slack, at
washed out coffee shade of
mansion flowing past, followed by
a washed out mustard old
museum. Our eyelids weigh
too much - oh see, that washed out
toast hotel,
that faded carrot Grill - our
throats have lumps, the eyeballs
prick - that Trattoria's shade
of camel.

Pass weighty plaster of the Rialto bridge.
A gondola looms the other way. The wife
stares woodenly ahead, while husband
in expensive specs, on mobile phone
checks index of the yen.

Moira Duff

FEAR

Fear is black
It tastes like burnt toast
and smells of smoke
fears look dark
the sound of heavy footsteps
fear is sad

Thomas McIlroy (6)

UNCONDITIONAL SURRENDER

The daily routine of toil and trial,
put here by my own lack of understanding.
Do I become involved to an excessive level,
so as to die in a state of unfulfilled selfish necessity.

Who is to become laudable in this world of repressive gesture.
Be shallow, be full, one as well as the other is insufficient;
so as to breed despair in one's self, and attract unkindly attention.
from peoples unknown to you in any form of friendship.

Be strong and push,
no barrier strong enough to hold you and pin you
to your existence of conditional ignorance.

Reach and grab a strand of a larger plausible direction in life
Inevitability from a young age,
might as well not participate in any of it.

Dreams of my own not of yours, ignore and disassemble my mind.
Like vultures above awaiting the stench of death,
you stalk and terrify me,
so as to drive me into a corner of senseless existence.

Hope for myself and those around who suffer as I do,
in a pit of ignorant beings
Looking at us as the zoo-keeper's latest attraction.

Paul Welsh

COLOURS OF MY LIFE

Pink - a girl, God's gift to Marion and Frank
For my life, the two of you I thank
Grey -confused, bewildered in unhappy ways
Dad's illness overshadowed childhood days
Black - the day we lost him, how I cried
No-one to love me, nowhere to hide
Pink - a girl, God's gift to Rosie and Chris
My Tracy, how I thank you God for this
Blue - relationships that always fell apart
One or other always had a failing heart
Red - passion abounding, hope in my breast
Always optimistic, always full of zest
Green - spring has turned to summer, prime of life
I now no longer want to be anyone's wife
Gold - something special, something untold
Finally finding someone to hold
Rainbow colours, glimpses of my past
In God's great mirage, I'll rest at last

Roseanna May

PAISLEY GOOD

It nestled at the bottom of the Glennifer Braes
A medieval Hamlet. Rolling in a feint blue haze
It crept up to a village then became a town
'Twas so flourishing and prosperous, jealous
Neighbours done it down.

Survival's been its forte throughout innumerable conflicts
Turning out quality, turning back countless dirty tricks
We've turned out shawls, we've churned out bombs
With conscientiousness, dignity, pride and even songs.

Elevated to a burgh by our great and gracious Queen
With parties and celebrations of a like never seen
We may be slightly prudish but never fuddy duddy
These ingredients are imperative to be a Paisley buddie.

Margaret Mary McVitie

TOO HARD

Too hard to handle
Too much to take
Too little a boat
To cross that lake

Too far to go
Too long to wait
To worry, am I
Too soon, too late

Too many problems
Too little time
Too many criminals
Too much crime

Too tired to walk
Too scared to stop
Too hard to climb
To the top

Too little am I
To make the choice
Too ignorant they are

To hear my voice

Sharon McLaughlin

PEACE?

I shudder at my thoughts today of man's inhumanity
To all creation, great or small it seems no matter what may befall,
Like wars, destruction, annihilation, causing fear and consternation
To all that live upon this Earth. Life now appears of little worth.

As if there's not enough to grieve, Beelzebub, his web does weave
By succour from his evil crew.
Mankind will his bidding do,
With death or ruin and no fear of cost we face the greatest Holocaust
This world of ours shall understand. Yet curing this is in our hands.

Why should we let a man insane run amok within Dunblane?
Widespread havoc upon his mind, reasons for which are hard to find,
Yet we as civil beings swear it's best we show them how we care
And leave them in Society to murder freely whilst they may.

It may be best we do not know, how these decisions are taken, so
That evil creatures can roam wild to cause our world to be defiled
By the actions that they take. It's time, I feel that we should break
For better or for worse, to rid our world of this evil curse.

One eye, an eye, one tooth, a tooth, from in the Bible we learn the truth
That causing harm to one another, is stealing from your very brother.
So let's not fool ourselves that we are secure and can live free,
As this malignancy in our veins, has happened to us yet again.

Civilisation must take the stand, amoral guns should *all* be banned
So we may live in harmony with all creation, to feel free
Of fear and apprehension, to live our lives without the tension.
Then wars and murders all shall cease to let us live our lives in *Peace*.

M J Blount

IRONIC

A dragon spurring
water you drink
the all powerful,
the wicked,
the killer instinct
Watching a ballet dancer
out on the ice rink
Like a writer writing
with no ink

Talk to me the deaf
boy cries
a blind man looks
with no eyes
A boy suffering a
common neurosis
turning the world
to a bloody psychosis
A police light bares
down from the sky
It's just authority
saying its goodbye
the witches' voices are
unmasked and sacred
like a house fire
burning naked

Tie your horrible thoughts
onto a barbed wire fence
        and like this poem,
        it makes no sense.

Steven McCredie

TOO HIGH!

The eagle rides the stars,
>love by his sides.
The serpent above,
>the secret of time, he hides.

Man rides the serpent
>Time in his soul,
nothing real, in his head.
>Love below, but not yet dead.

The reality of similar things.
>getting so, so close.
The barriers between
>soon to spring apart.

The meaning for now lost,
>thought has a terrible cost.
The mind so often blown,
>too, too often sanity has flown.

The will to die, comes here.
>Flown too high, you're too near
Trust leaves this place
>Has anyone, one face?

Keith Church

THOUGHTS OFA BRITISH SERVICEMAN ON OVERSEAS DUTY IN EGYPT 1947

On the banks of the Suez canal he lay, his forehead brown and furrowed.
Whilst only just a foot away, the ants they scraped and burrowed.

His thoughts they carried him o'er the waves to find that land so far away
To that loyal town of the royal crown
And the valley wherein it lay.

126

Once more he saw the roses grow round that trellised gate
And his mind's eye could picture the gardener's greying pate.
His thoughts were of his parents then. He wondered how they fared.
And of his childhood sweetheart, he wondered if she cared.

But soon he awoke to reality, the Suez at his feet.
And at his back the rolling sands still shimmered in the heat.

John Stark

SKYE AT EASTER '96

As we cross the bridge,
I suddenly realise where I am.
A couple of seconds away
from the place I've been dreaming of for months.
I get all excited and sit up on my chair,
I squeeze my teddies as if I were worried,
no, but I'm excited.
I sit back and take in all the magnificent scenery,
as we pass Sligachan,
the Cuillins are covered in mist.
We get to the hill-farm
and it's cold and dark.
Dad unhitches the caravan and the next minute
I'm lying snug in the caravan bed
in the sleeping bag.
We sit in the Cuillin Hills hotel for a relaxing
bar supper.
We eat our lunch in Aros and talk about what
we're going to do for the next couple of days.
Hours become seconds,
days become minutes
and we're back home
unloading the caravan
Back to the old routine!

Katie Green (10)

BROKEN

Surround me with impenetrable walls,
Entomb me with these fears.
Obliged to grant you anything.
Embalm my soul with tears.
Cast me from this barren ground
With dreams that are obscure
Mutilate my sacred temple
And I'll be yours no more.

Jo Clarke

AYRSHIRE

We live in a county
that's small and clean
Ayrshire's its name
It has to be seen

Its history is famous
For poets and more
To go through Ayrshire
Will lead to a shore

Its towns are quaint
Its shops are famous
For high class quality
and sweaters famous
so come along and see
what we've got
We may be small
but we've got a lot.

Caron Walker

MY NEW WELLIES

I wanted a pair of wellies when I was a little lass
A pair that went up to my knees
no puddles would I pass
My friend she had a yellow pair
and I was green all over
She would jump in every puddle
as I would quietly hover
So I went to see my Mam
and for a pair I pleaded
I went on about them every day
until finally she heeded
She promised me I'd have a pair
when I got home from school
All day I just sat dreaming
not of puddles now but pools
I couldn't wait to get there
I rushed and ran real fast
I looked at all the puddles, at last I'd get to splash
I dashed into the house
and quickly through the door
and there was my new wellies sitting on the floor
They were red and shiny
and nice I would agree,
but there was one big problem, they were way below my knees
Little ankle wellies my Mam had gone and bought
Little ankle wellies no puddles would I sought
So on went those wee wellies
and outside I went to play
to watch my friend with her yellow ones
jump in puddles all the day.

K Feeney

AGINCOURT BOWMAN

You taught me how to draw.
How to lay my body
in my bow.
And not to draw with simple
strength of arms but with strength
of mind.

You brought me bows
according to my age
and mental strength.
As I increased in them, so you
made me bows bigger and more exacting
in their kind

For men, you said,
shall never shoot well
or straight.
Save they are brought up to it.

Trevor L Hutchinson

CONCLUSIONS ON MY MIND

As the quiet begins and my concerns start to arise,
I imagine my life, a world without lies,
It would be full of the dreams I thought I'd foreseen,
No time for reminiscing, things that could have been.

My head would have no turmoil, trauma and tragedy,
Replaced with love and laughter, the important things to me,
With a touch of comfort and kindness, a sense so complete,
To give it all a meaning, a belief in what I seek.

And to have these simple thoughts of which never to forget,
Looking only on good times, to have not a regret,
So with this kind of feelings I know that I will find,
No longer do I have confusion but conclusions on my mind.

Carol M Walker

THE GARDENER'S TRIBUTE

The slumbering garden rests in deep repose
As if in silent mourning.
Yesterday's gifted hands that wrought perfection here
Will tend no more
These manicured lawns of emerald green,
Nor cup a summer bloom
With petals delicate as a butterfly's wing,
Nor ever pluck
A blushing apple from the autumn bough.
I remember him
As, in a mist of memories I ramble now
Along well-trimmed paths
That stretch like ribbons - neat-edged, weed-free,
I linger and reflect
By the old garden bench, rustic and rude,
Embosomed
By kaleidoscopic colour, extravagant and bold.
The garden, now,
Serves as a timeless shrine;
A monument
To his eternal artistry and skill.
His toil is done.
Wearily he slumbers, akin once more
With his beloved soil.

Ann Richard

DUNBLANE

My dreams are haunted
by your evil image.
A raving mad-man going
to the school and taking
those young lives.
I see their blood dripping
from their bodies and into
the newspaper headlines.
The families in grief and
the world shocked by
the heartless killings.
I pray for those lost
souls and for the families
left behind
and wish this was another
bad dream.

J Beaumont

WAVES

Against the promenade they crash,
Gently hitting the rocks they splash.
So ferocious, they send a chill down my spine,
The world is my oyster, but this ocean is mine.

I see the sea, when it's bright and blue,
And I watch it when it's dark and grey,
I touch the waves, when they come so close,
And I watch them take my thoughts away.

When I live in an ocean of unrequited love,
And my heart is sinking to the bottom of the sea,
I go and watch my precious waves
And they bring my heart right back to me.

Diane McEvoy McCall

ADVENTURES OF A WHALE

On bended knees I pray to you
Come, listen to my tale
It takes place in the ocean blue
- 'Adventures of a whale'.

As stars were shining bright one night
He wanted to be near
And so grew forth some wings of flight
(A wish he'd held so dear)

He flew around the universe
And kissed each twinkling star
And with the Planets he'd converse
And strum on his guitar

Saturn sang a song of love
The whale, he shed a tear
He never dreamt that life above
Could e'er be so sincere

He fluttered slowly to the moon
And spoke about his fear
That in the sea comes Man's harpoon
But why? - He wasn't clear

The planets vowed to watch upon
All whales down in the ocean
So if they saw Man do more wrong
They'd put the land in motion

So if you ever see the whale
With head out of the sea
Remember this my little tale
And leave the creature be.

T O'Rourke

MEG'S HOOSE

It stands upon the brae, forlorn,
of sandstone grey, Carmyllie born.
The Fairlie fields bear winter's sheen
of barley breared, resplendent green,
and oil-seed rape's firm-rooted stocks,
a tempting lure to pigeon flocks.

The winter day breaks dank and chill
as sun lies hid 'neath Downie hill.
That lazy January globe
reluctant frees its rays to probe
the Northern Sea's grey, foaming swell
and Angus shore wind-beaten, snell.

Celestial rhythm keeps its beat.
The dull-red globe sends forth its heat.
The ruddy glow's now orange-bright.
It crests the hill and sheds its light
full on the panes of Meg's wee hoose.
The Bell rock beam could scarce produce
the dazzling fire's reflected glare.
At breakfast, I just sit and stare.
Have walls and roof of cottar hame
been vitrified by Phoebus' flame?

The minutes tick away, alas!
The hands of Heaven's clock must pass
and with them change the angled beam.
The window-panes no longer gleam.
Meg's hoose stands on the brae, forlorn,
of sandstone grey, Carmyllie born.

Don Smith

MYSTERY OF LIFE

The man in the moon and the wind in the hair
The pretty young girl sits by the chair
Dreams in her head of what one day may be
The reality of her destiny.
The roar of the lion, the bleat of the lamb
The coldness of death, the peace and the calm,
The joy in the warmth of the sun on the skin
New-born babes set to begin
The journey through life, the cycles go round
The gurgling of streams, routes newly found
On the towering mountains, who no-one may claim
Caught in a trap, the deer now is lame.
The river is racing its way to the sea
The leaves turn to gold and soon it will be
Cold and barren, bereft of beauty
They soldier on, aware of their duty
To keep the peace, a balance bring
To lands far away where none now sing,
Wounded and weary, the wages of war
All losers, no winners, what's it all for?
The rage of the bear, step on its patch
The fury and fervour, no-one may match
Thunder and lightning to chill to the bone
The strength of mankind, to look after his own.
The sun filters through a cloudy sky
To cheer the spirit, to still the cry
But certain wounds they never heal
Such is life, time will reveal.

Jacqueline D Rhodes

NOTICING

I sat and watched and wondered why,
The cows in the meadow and the pigs in the sty,
And all the rest could get by,
Without really noticing things like I,
Things that make me laugh and things that make me cry,
And so it will always be until the day I die.

I'd get so down I'd sometimes sigh,
Occasionally there would be sadness in my eye,
And often when a far away look would descend,
I'd think of old times and I'd start to mend,
I'd remember when I began to notice,
I'd remember the joy of noticing I could notice.

I'd remember my mother would say to me,
Son go out and find a tree,
Find a tree in a wood,
Sit down and be good,
Be good and look around,
At the world you have found.

And when clear thoughts spring to mind,
Write them down and you will find,
Find upon reflection one day,
That the world has wonderful things to say,
Wonderful things create wonderful feelings,
Absorb them and use them in your dealings.

Notice how others notice the pleasure,
A person gets when he notices life's treasure,
Notice how others then begin more to notice,
A world full of interesting things to notice,
Notice how they then pass on the dictum,
About noticing to others who notice them . . . Ad infinitum.

Tom McQuenn

CAPE HORN

Bleak, dark and bare,
this unremarkable rock
has borne the ceaseless shock
of wind and wave
since first Pacific gave
its foaming, tumbling traffic
to the Atlantic.

Scar on a continent's heel,
known only to the lonely seal
and a searching, hungry gull,
whose dive, white from the dull
black sky, scatters fish among
the weed-strung, broken
bones of ships and men.

Slowly, this, the offset pole
of the doomed earth turns
as the flickering hate burns
from East to West;
until the final test
splits the world's belly, spilling
life, and leaving . . .

Gull-men, metempsychotic,
tilling the earthless rock?
or this bare, unnurtured cape
alone in the hard Antarctic night.

W Stewart Wallace

CONFLICT

Killing, screaming, hurting, bleeding.
The innocent die. They are the true epitaph to our mindless
activities.
The living; dying reflection of our hostility.
War seldom hurts the delegates,
But scars the people who stand by waiting for peace, for a
better era, for a life free from misery and contempt.
All are torn apart by hatred and the hurt.
They look on, they watch the exploding mortar fire, the
devastating blow to themselves, to their families.
Both sides look on, the world acknowledges the horror, comforted by
the fact that 'We can't do anything'.
Both sides cry for the land they've lost,
And the peace,
Their families now shattered and divided.

We premeditate this kind of torture,
These guns serve a double purpose.
They witness both sides;
They kill, they protect, they manifest fear . . .
Children are the victims this time.

Karen McGavock

UND JEDEN TAG GEHEN WIR AN EINEM MORD VORBEI

A child is being murdered
Slowly and silently
Without repent
Soon no-one will know
It ever was.

The child knows
But it is too late to tell
So it accepts its plight
It can do no other

As time is closing in
The child in its complete despair
Can derive its final pleasure
In spectating its own obliteration
Even finally, in completing it itself.

Kvétka Jirásková

ST CHRISTOPHER'S CITY

The cathedral city with dreaming spires
And the blood of St Christopher on its hands,
It maybe a historical fiction and its diction Latin
But the sins of their deeds are cast ash-like in the
spirited air

The tombs with sculpted effigies
Living emblems of bony dust and decay
'O' Lord they said when your kingdom came into view
The town was not worthy of such bounty

The ghost of Jesus Christ rose here in medieval times
Thus, pilgrims squat and genuflect at the sacred site
And at the university scholars pore over books
Predicting this sign as the end of the millennium

Breeding religion absorbed the market villagers' minds
St Christopher was a heretic the prophets declare
Smash the stone, chisel into his memory
Kill your idol dead!

Not a scent, not a trace exists of his name in records
The blood of St Christopher is on their hands
Apologies sent from angels and cherubs to the dethroned
God is in heaven and so it shall always be.

Alistair Tankard

SECURITY THE ELUSIVE DREAM

Somehow there is no permanency,
And yet on sunny days,
When birds sing and flowers smile,
Yes through that haze
There is a continuity of style.

Security the elusive dream,
It comes, it goes,
Almost within reach, but not quite
It keeps one awake through many a night,
It's there, where? The chance arose,
Or was it just a dream again.

Tomorrow, I say tomorrow,
No more fears, no more tears,
Tomorrow, I say tomorrow,
What was that eh! The passing of the years,
Tomorrow is today.

Jeanne McChlery

THE WHEEL OF STEEL

Seven chimneys black and cold,
Stark against the twilight sky,
Seven chimneys black and cold,
Reminders of an age gone by.

The great dark shed is now deserted,
Once the womb of new born steel,
Silence broods within its portals,
Silence that one's soul can feel,

The last tap now is part of history,
And with it all the men have gone,
Ingot moulds, discarded ladles,
Life abandoned all forlorn.

Soon will come the breakers' torches,
Scything all before their flame,
The wheel of steel has turned full circle,
Back to scrap from whence it came.

Robert Lynn

DEATH OF A PRINCIPLE

First the jeering and then the cheering
Pain dispensed, in the sun blessed clearing.
Hang on in there, things will get brighter
What comfort now the Consul's words
Drowned out by a new Air Force fighter

Do what they say, don't say what they do
Think what you like, don't do it out loud
Good advice, when wrapped in a shroud
Insular, secretive, xenophobic community
It's not for me this oppressive lunacy

Drank a beer in the midday sun
A beautiful girl admired in passing
For God's sake that's all I done
Too late now to hide and run
Crimes I've committed, guilty bar none

Ministers pronounce - a contract procured
Safe guarding jobs and incomes secured
But for my blasphemous sins that fateful day
Fourteen days and one hundred strokes
This was the price that I had to pay

A G McTaggart

OUR DAILY PAIN

Mes cheries are you aware?
Do you realise the perils abound.
Is it that you easily scare,
or are your feet firmly on the ground.

Our food chain is direly threatened,
we are daily bombarded by pessimists.
Doom and gloom ascertained
by scientists and environmentalists.

What are we to do in our quests
for equanimity in our daily lives.
Do we label our informers - pests
for disturbing our forks and knives.

Should we abandon our daily bread,
refuse to fill our delicate gullet
when each morning we quit our bed.
The quandary is really quite the limit.

Shall we feel ill and faint
for want of sustenance - the staff of life.
Or shall we risk the taint,
inviting ailments which are rife.

Food that may be contaminated
tempts our unsuspecting palate.
Tasty dishes deliciously marinated
may accelerate us to cremate.

Let us all just take our chances
savour succulent steaks and vegetable terrine,
sugar, spice and all that enhances.
Ah vive la francais cuisine.

Rebecca Strangward

JUST A MEMORY

An eternity has passed.
Apart for so long,
but you've never completely left my mind.
I can imagine you, instantly,   ·
your face demanding respect,
but still a picture of glory.

Your memory lingers in my mind.
Your ever busy mind and body,
never ceasing to amaze those surrounding you.
Steadily producing new thoughts
and new inspiration.
Inserting knowledge into the minds of generations new.

Someone thought always to be there,
no longer life, just a memory.
The highest branch of the tree,
suddenly broken,
leaving younger shoots
grieving for your mature experience.

The reality, of your memory,
calming and almost explaining,
soothing the grief, controlling the pain.
You will always be there in my mind,
protecting all your offspring,
your loving memory carries on.

Claire Dick

THE GRIEF OF DAFFODILS
(To Stewart in memory of Dunblane)

The knowledge that life exists
      outside this darkness,
Is not dormant but
      unnaturally delayed.

The cold earth oppresses me,
Deluding me that my future
lies only
Wrapped in its clammy grasp.

Why should I bloom, golden
When others decay
Plucked in a second?

A memory haunts me and
I cry.
Tears?
Or raindrops from above?
Powerless to resist the process of growth,
I reluctantly sense the warmth.
Soon I will know the pain of breaking through
Only to realise I stand among
a carpet of golden blooms.

But as we bow our heads to the passing breeze
the raindrops will still trickle.

Lorna Sabbagh

THE OLD LADY

Alone she sits so poor and cold
No friends she has, so I've been told,
A fire I could hold in my hand,
I'm sure she's in no happy land.

But determination keeps her alive,
It's amazing how she does survive,
To think she is so unfortunate
And nothing to her is a fate.

Thin hands she has, and blue with cold,
How bad it is when you grow old,
No company or love to share,
Nobody gives for her a care.

Long black dress, cape on her back,
Warm shoes she does lack,
Stockings thin, darns here and there,
Few pins and net keep in her hair.

A face so grey her eyes sunk in,
Her cheeks hang down so very thin,
Glasses rest upon her nose,
Sitting quite happy while she sews.

At night while she lies in her bed,
Many a thought goes through her head,
She thinks of the gone by days,
And good health is for what she prays.

Sheila Irvine Fraser Wann

NOURISH

Gentle hopes worry
            at the stuff of self-contempt;
Flowers possibly blooming
            in the sustenance
            of good intent,
            Cheery smiles and
            unsullied confidences.
Words. Are only words.
            but still,
There's meanings in dictionaries . . .
And then there's meanings more . . .
Beyond the frigid stuff of
            definition, cynicism,
There is a little laugh
            Which,
Amplified by gentle wish
            and well-meant words,
Can flower through the briars.
And even open colourfully wide-eyed
            in the suppressing shade
Of politicians, cheats and liars.

Douglas Baird

TO A MIDGE

On warm humid nights
When the temperature's just right
On water boat or bridge
You'll find the Scottish midge.

Most people come to stay
With cream and nets and spray
A few become immune
But most stay in their room.

Foreigners and natives too
Do not know just what to do
To rid the nation of each itch
And drive away the Scottish midge.

But we could not do without
That wee fly that makes us shout
It is like Nessie, as you'll see
It's in all Highland History.

Alison Niven

WITCH WIFE

Lightning splits the darkened sky,
Thunder rolls across the glen,
From the north, a piercing cry,
Mag the witch is passing by.

Crooked nose and pointed face,
Offspring of a bygone race,
Moaning, groaning, casting spells,
Crying, sighing, ringing bells.

Mag casts the seventh eye far seeing,
From whose gaze are kelpies fleeing,
Weaving spells and magic potions,
Stirring up those evil notions.

Skulls are hanging from the door,
Secret signs upon the floor,
By the fire Mag sits waiting,
In her hands a doll impaling.

Evening shadows gently falling,
Suddenly a voice is calling,
Reindeer scatter below the Ben
Mag the witch-wife's in her den.

James Adams

WHAT A FRIEND IS FOR

A friend is someone you can turn to,
When you no longer feel you can cope,
They will hold your hand, listen to you,
Give a smile, and give you hope,
For they too have gone through this life,
Their ups and downs they've bared,
How grateful they are also to you
For the time you both have shared,
When you're down they'll help pick you up
When you're sad, they'll make you smile,
All these things a friend will do,
To make life more worthwhile.

Valerie Eagleson

AUTUMN ARRIVES

Autumn arrives
 With the wind and rain
  Leaves on the rails
   Winter is a pain
    Frozen points on the track
     causing upset to the train
      Summer on the way
       at last
        Leaves on the trees
         Frozen points things of
          the past
           Trains should be on
            Time *again*!

Lorna McNeil

148

TOY BOYS

Remember the days as a slight young lassie
Full of spirit, bright and sassy
Pert wee figures forming softly
Passions surging uncontrollably

Those thoughts of lust were made in ignorance
The acts performed lacked all the substance
The fumbled ways we set in motion
Those teenage thoughts, virgin notions

Remember the lads all sweaty and spotty
Those older men who drove us dotty
We dreamt of the men but chased the boys
Practising on them as if they were toys

Thinking of that first performance
Heavy petting and panting, not lacking endurance
But the speed of the act left me feeling disturbed
It was almost as if it had never occurred

I realise now it was all lack of experience
No real feeling or meaning - just purely experiments
But I shall never regret my easy ways
They were part and parcel of those learning days.

Caroline Murray

MUSIC

Music is a symphony of melodious phrase,
Of Beethoven and Schubert those were the days,
When music was music,
A note was a note,
Mystical sounds on the air they would float,
Progressing through the ages and ages of song,
From classical to pop,
We still go on,
From blue to jazz,
From rock to soul,
From Elvis to Handl, Madonna and more,
Although we still play it isn't the same,
It's only progression, there's no-one to blame,
I suppose there's a rhythm we beat out the time,
On the great drum of the world that's both yours and mine,
The great drum will beat softly for others to hear,
High over the crowds it will sound loud and clear,
But however loud and clear it may be,
To all of us it's plain to see,
It may have come it may have gone,
But at least we're assured it will live on.

Fiona McNab

OLD COLLEGE ROOM REVISITED

My memories were locked behind this door -
My old lamp, angled tidily away,
My bed, made up with pristine sheets today,
A wine stain left on sprucely hoovered floor.

In that chair smiled a girlfriend, now long gone,
I've made my mark in mug-rings on that desk,
Now see, through stiff uncurtained emptiness,
That view of slates and windy trees beyond.

But this neat empty room is mine no more,
So sadly old, reluctant, I retreat
And notice as I do my shoe soles squeak
That same way all along the corridor.

Stephen Blease

MOTHER AND FATHER
(I NEVER MEANT TO HURT YOU)

Mother and Father, Mum and Dad
Please listen to what I have to say
I've stolen from you, I've lied to you
That's the second worse thing I've done to you
I turned to drugs and know how that hurt you
That's the worst thing I've ever done to you
But I just can't find the words in my head
To say how sorry I am, just how sorry I am
And please believe me, I never meant to hurt you
I never meant to hurt the way I have
After all the things you have done for me
For putting up with and still loving me
When I had no place to go
You took me in and looked after me
So for all you have done 'Thank you'
And know I will always love you
But I just can't find the words in my head
To say how sorry I am for what I put you through
I want you to remember
I love you both more than anything, more than anything
I never meant to hurt you
No I never meant to hurt you.

Kenneth Thornton

THE COLD LIGHT OF DAY

There's a million and one complications
of the heart, at the start.
There's a thousand and one mixed sensations
when we part, when we part.
There are stars in the skies, like the
stars in your eyes, now they've gone
all faded away.
But the colours in my mind, and my dreams
now I find, have gone with the
cold light of day.
I have wandered alone,
with my heavy heart of stone
looking for some comfort, here and there.
As I stop to unwind
just ease off my mind,
with a view, and a glass
of light beer.
Now I'm on the road again
just looking for a friend,
there's a sea of faces everywhere.
Some are black, some are white,
all strangers in daylight,
but I know most of them don't care.
I've been many faces,
seen lots of places,
never wanted to stay.
Then shades become clearer as
day draws nearer,
This is the cold light of day.

B Vidovic

GIN I WIR YOUNG

Gin I wir young again
And dauchlin by the burn
Watchin' silver fishes weave and flash.
past polished stanes and waving rash.

Tae lie abeen the grassy bank and feel
The warm sunlicht on my face
And watch the white chargers race across
the sky, and disappear fae trace.

Tae tak the path tae the Craggen Ben
An' feel the win' caress my face
And watch the soaring eagles float
high in majestic grace.

Tae wanner through the wids of autumn glory
Canopied in gold's and russet re-eds
An' try and grasp the golden rays o' sunlicht
Streaming through the trees
Tae let, them slip through my fingers
Like jewelled silken threeds.

Sine winter frosts and icy win's
Like auld age comes alang
An' a' I've left are memories
Of treasured youth lang gane.

L H McIntosh

FAULTLESS LOVE

We stood together on the north pier
and looked out across the bay,
we could see the cliffs of the Buchan coast
over a sea so grey.

I passed my weight
to the arms of an angel
and floated above the day,
it was not a dream,
but a faultless love,
that carried me away.

Now as I lie here next to you
and watch you slowly breathe,
I wonder what it is you find
when you look inside of me.

I passed my weight
to the arms of an angel
to be forgiven as I forgave
it was not a dream,
but a faultless love,
that carried me away.

I lost myself
in what remained of the night,
to sleep and then awake,
this time should last eternally
for love's sweet enchanted sake.

R A Fraser

LITTLE ANGELS

Little angels holding hand
'All through the night'
Going to the golden sands
'All through the night'
People asking why oh why
Little children have to die
The nation weeps, while parents cry
All through the night

Little flowers blooming bright
All through the night
Twinkling stars, a ray of light
All through the night
Heaven above is where they are
Forget me nots is what they are
They, will shine on every star
'All through the night

Bless the children one, by one
All through the night
Someone's daughter, someone's son
All through the night
God be with them in Dunblane
Only he can heal their pain
Till at last they meet again
All through the night

Dot Niven

FINAL CURTAIN

Born in Zanzibar, who would have thought,
that this little boy, could so easily have brought,
such marvel and inspiration into everyone's mind.
Magic, harmony, every song lined
with shining ample gold.

Such a gift, given from the Gods above.
He was an original, filling everyone's heart with true love.
Not even the most, visualised pray
has the power to give him back his life, that was unfairly
snatched, from his hand.
I hope he is now in a safer and contented land!

Freddie Mercury!
No words are able to describe him so.
This man was a genius,
but, he had to let go,
and as his final curtain closed
he took one deep breath,
and his spirit and soul rose.

Adele E McCafferty

A FAREWELL

Farewell my love for here I go
my heart belongs to distant shores,
I dreamt I had the wanderlust
and will remember, and I must,
the ache and pain I left in you.

For I was young and did refuse
to give my heart and love to you,
the urge to see a different land,
was my refusal to hold your hand,
I prayed you found another love.

Your hopes were great when we said goodbye,
in years that passed you wonder why
you ever felt this way for me,
as happiness you found with her,
who now loves and cares for you each day.

H Kolonko

ROSEBUDS
'REMEMBER THE CHILDREN'

These rosebuds will one day open
The gardener never works in vain,
And how he'll love those children
Now he's called them home again,
His garden is well tended
For he watches every flower,
And what happened on that morning
Must have been his darkest hour.

His flowers were all scattered,
Not by a weed, we dare not say,
For a weed is just a flower,
That has simply gone astray.

But the gardener will care for them
As he will you and me
And when those rosebud's open
They'll be happy, safe and free.

Elizabeth McKinlay

THE DANCING DOLLS

Day gives way to nightfall and all its advantages
are there to be taken, it's time, time to leave
Our concrete tents of its working day. We move silently
but our thoughts are loud with the thought of our destination.
The bending roads and piercing lights lead us to our
recreational destination and a variety of wondrous strangers
come into view. The tent sits like a monster with
no end to its hunger for people that are lead
through its mouth, and as we enter our silence
is shattered by a climax of sound that echoes our future.
Our only means of escape is to fly as high as the
eagle mentally and spiritually but without wings
for tonight we take flight and let Lucy leave the
doors open.
Sleep is but a dream, our bodies move like broken
puppets surrounded by piercing black eyes like those
of a doll. Why are we here, what is this feeling
that haunts us like a demon possessing our body
that we play host to. Our only fear is that
of the black hatters who would come and break
this spell.
As night starts to fade our hearts still rage with
the music, but it's time to break the spell. Tomorrow
gives us new dreams of life and reality we
must be ready.

Alistair Ross